D1631697

The Writing School

Also by Miranda France

NON-FICTION

Bad Times in Buenos Aires
Don Quixote's Delusions: Travels in Castilian Spain

FICTION

That Summer at Hill Farm
The Day Before the Fire

The Writing School

Miranda France

corsair

CORSAIR

First published in the United Kingdom in 2023 by Corsair

1 3 5 7 9 10 8 6 4 2

Copyright © 2023, Miranda France

The moral right of the author has been asserted.

This is a memoir, however the participants described in the 'Writing School' chapters are invented and some other events, settings and characters have been fictionalised.

All rights reserved.
No part of this publication may be reproduced, stored in a
retrieval system, or transmitted, in any form or by any means, without
the prior permission in writing of the publisher, nor be otherwise circulated
in any form of binding or cover other than that in which it is published
and without a similar condition including this condition being
imposed on the subsequent purchaser.

The extract on page 47 is from 'Widows', in *William Trevor: The Collected Stories*, William Trevor (Penguin, London, 2003). Reproduced with permission of Johnson & Alcock Ltd.

The extract on page 47 is from *Bad Blood*, Lorna Sage (Fourth Estate, 2001). Reprinted with permission of HarperCollins Publishers Ltd © (*Lorna Sage*) (*2001*).

The acknowledgements on pp. 197–211 constitute an extension of this copyright page.

A CIP catalogue record for this book is available from the British Library.

ISBN: 978-1-4721-5734-8

Typeset in Caslon by M Rules

Printed and bound in Great Britain by Clays Ltd, Elcograf S.p.A.

Papers used by Corsair are from well-managed forests and other responsible sources.

Corsair
An imprint of
Little, Brown Book Group
Carmelite House
50 Victoria Embankment
London EC4Y 0DZ

An Hachette UK Company
www.hachette.co.uk

www.littlebrown.co.uk

For Richard

'I always just assumed the important
things would stay somehow, but they don't'

JAMES SALTER,
Light Years

Contents

Day One: Writing School   1

Exercise One: A Sense of Place   26

Day Two: Writing School   48

Exercise Two: Keeping A Diary   80

Day Three: Writing School   117

Exercise Three: Writing from Life   140

Day Four: Writing School   164

Endings   187

A Note on Sources   197

Day One

Writing School

Always *get there before the others.* Why hadn't I remembered that from the last time? If you arrive a few hours early there's time to go for a walk, arrange your room as you like it and to start building the persona of a writer, the first creative exercise of the week. We don't teach in our bedrooms any more – it's either too dangerous or too tempting – but the manuscripts begin arriving early on. They may be pushed under the bedroom door. Or under the bathroom door. There are no boundaries the aspiring writer is not prepared to breach.

The first time I was asked to teach a creative writing course I couldn't believe my luck. Four days in lovely scenery, with someone else to cook my meals? That didn't sound like something you should get paid for. Writing courses usually take place in beautiful locations, on Greek islands, in the hills or by the sea. And the trouble with beauty, my fellow tutor told me that week, is that it encourages people to produce the kind of writing they would never want to read themselves. 'Please let me never have to read another poem about the mournful gaze of a sheep.' He thought it would be better to teach writing in industrial parks and shopping centres, the places where people actually spend their days, so that they learned to observe and describe their own lives, not some bucolic ideal. Would anyone want to spend a week's holiday on an industrial estate, though? Perhaps the solution was to stay somewhere beautiful, with excursions into the 'real world' – day trips to car plants and abattoirs, the would-be writers touring pig carcasses or Peugeots and learning to see how things are made, and unmade.

Writing courses have come a long way, all the same, since they started in the 1970s. Tales handed down from those times tell of free spirits sharing food and basic provisions, running naked through fields, sleeping with the tutors and each other. 'Shagathon' was the word a friend of mine used to describe a typical early course, though she had probably fallen for the mythology. These days creaking floorboards in the night more likely signal a weak bladder than anything sexual. Sooner or later the hippieish model had been tamed by a code of conduct; those free spirits wanted to get published, after all. Britain might not yet have a Creative Writing industry to match that of the United States, worth hundreds of millions of dollars, but there's a growing demand, and money to be made even from a half day taught by a midlist author.

I should have arrived earlier, but this year I visited a friend on the way and ended up stepping off the train at the same time as some of the people attending the course I was about to teach. I recognized them immediately. They radiated the mild anxiety that attends all residential courses. It was already palpable on the platform. By midweek it would reach a peak and someone might decide to leave. 'Wednesday is the danger day,' my first cotutor warned me. The triggers had changed, as life itself had changed, over the fifteen years I'd been teaching. On that first course, snoring roommates were the main complaint. Nowadays few people share rooms, but lots more of them worry about what they eat or what they say.

Now six of us stood in the station car park, looking at a taxi that could only take four. The driver said that he could call a friend with a van, but it would take half an hour to arrive. Two young women, stylishly dressed in charity shop finds, offered to wait for the second taxi while the rest of us went on ahead. Even this was going to be difficult because Peter, a tall man in his late seventies who used a walking stick, couldn't easily be accommodated in the low-slung front seat. The taxi driver kneeled into his car, half an inch of arse reddening above his waistband as he pulled at levers until the passenger seat was thrust back. Eventually, I wedged myself into the space behind it, my holdall with

3

everything I needed for the next five days pressed against my face.

As we drove along cobbled streets, then off onto a road that wound into the hills, the others described their journeys, which had been the usual mixture of delays and difficult connections. I looked out of the window, thinking how universal an opener it was to ask strangers where they had come from. The Queen famously started conversations this way, although my son said South London gangsters often asked where you were from, too, before advising you to stick to your own postcode. I kept quiet, annexed by my own bag, until someone asked if anyone knew about the tutors. In all the confusion over taxis I had half-forgotten that I was here to teach.

I peered through a gap from behind my bag, like Jack Nicholson smiling through the space where his axe had been. 'Yes,' I said. 'I'm one of them.'

'Oh,' said the woman next to me. 'You don't look much like the photo in the booklet.'

'I expect it's a bit out of date.'

You can't help hoping, as a writer, that some quiet stardom may attach to your name. It's not that you want admiration, exactly, just an acknowledgement of the trials and the triumphs of the writing life. Most authors have had so much more experience of the former. They have sat at a table in a book shop or a festival tent and had no one come up to get their book signed. They have waited in the lavatories of provincial libraries, while an audience of eight people gathers to listen to a talk that will send two of them to sleep. I was once asked to sign a book that had WITHDRAWN FROM STOCK rubber-stamped all the way through it.

The taxi was climbing a steep hill now and Peter's head tipped back towards me, conveying the calm irritation of an air passenger on a sharp ascent. Then, as we reached the hill's summit, we took a left turn and descended just as sharply, my face thrust into my bag as the car swung into a drive beside a big house where car doors were slamming and cases being taken out of boots and there was a sense of people arriving at a house party to which not enough men had been invited. Two thirds of creative writing participants are female, a large proportion are over fifty and a small, but growing, number are not white.

The house-party analogy holds, despite these odd proportions, and even if this is a party where kitchen antics seem destined, at some point in the week, to overcome the parlour. We freed ourselves from the taxi and settled into the rooms that had been allocated to us. In mine there were flowers in a vase and two windows looking out onto a garden in full bloom. Later, over a dinner of lasagna, the new housemates talked volubly, the relief of safe arrival mixed with trepidation about the days ahead. Most of the people sitting at my end of the table had never formally studied creative writing before except for one shy-seeming man in his forties who said that he had been on a course the previous summer and enjoyed it so much he had decided immediately to sign up for another one. He mentioned the names of the writers who had taught him and I knew one of them.

'She's great. I hope I can be equally inspiring,' I said. He pushed his glasses up his nose and took a sip of wine. 'She set the bar high,' he said sombrely. Peter, my irritable taxi companion, asked if I had ever considered writing children's books – perhaps if I did I could become as successful as J. K. Rowling. I said that I hadn't considered it, but left the door open to the possibility that I might, now that he had put the idea into my head. There's always someone transfixed by the success of J. K. Rowling.

We had almost finished the lasagna by the time my cotutor Tom arrived, having walked up from the station in hiking boots, with a rucksack and a paperback sticking out of his pocket. Tom was a poet who had been compared to Ted Hughes and looked the part as he entered the dining room, ruddy with exertion and fresh air, drawing many admiring glances from around the table. His was much the best entrance of the evening.

The same spirit of relief and trepidation that had prevailed over supper carried us into the sitting room, where the participants had to introduce themselves and explain what they hoped to get out of the week. Three of the youngest members of the group, all in their twenties, had gathered on one sofa. They were Zoe and Kisi, the girls from the station, two friends who wanted to write about festival culture, and Sam, who had jacked in his job as a barman to spend a year travelling in South East Asia and hoped to turn his diary into a travelogue. On the next sofa were Peter, who wanted to write detective stories set in Roman Bath, and Diana, also in her seventies. She had found some letters belonging to an aunt in the attic and wondered if there were something she could do with them. Lily was a young Chinese–American woman who worked in the City as an insurance broker but liked journalling and wanted to engage more with her creative side. Next to her, Jules and Jim ('we've heard all the jokes') were a couple in their fifties who liked the idea of a country writing holiday, while Susie, sitting next to them, was interested in writing a memoir and wanted to be pushed out of her comfort zone. Beside her was Nick, the quiet man who had already done a course, and Lynn, who worked in Human Resources and 'just fancied something different'. Finally there was Sheena, a woman draped in fabric that seemed designed to trick the eye into some uncertainty over how much was fabric and how much Sheena.

'Is it my turn?' she asked, leaning forward with her glass of wine, as though to propose a toast. She said that she worked for 'the enemy', with an apologetic eye roll, and when none of us got the allusion, explained that she meant the Inland Revenue. Then she said that she had come on the course because five years ago her neighbour had tried to murder her, and she wanted to write a book about this ordeal.

Tom and I swapped our encouraging smiles for ones of

supportive concern. These are the two most useful expressions on a writing course, and quick changes between them are sometimes required.

'How absolutely dreadful,' said Susie.

'Yes,' Sheena said with a sigh, 'not my best moment.'

*

I had set my alarm to go off early. Waking up in a large shared house is like being returned to childhood: you sense the proximity of sleepers and wonder who will stir next, for how long you will be alone. I looked out of the window at the glimmering hills, thinking about going for a run. I was more interested in the concept of myself as the kind of person who went for a run before a day of teaching than in the running itself. But a writing course offers the chance of reinvention, for tutors as well students, and as long as my trainers were there, paired at the foot of my bed, it remained a possibility. Still in my pyjamas, I crept downstairs to make toast and a cafetière of coffee to take back up to my room. A stealth raid, hoping no one had got there first. Experience had taught me that I could be friendly over lunch and supper, but not at breakfast. 7 a.m. was too early for a conversation about getting published.

This was the first morning and the kitchen still had a fresh, organized look. Inside the fridge were cow's milk, almond milk, coconut milk, oat milk and soya milk along with spreads to cater for all tastes and dietary needs. All kinds of cereals and breads were lined up on the counter for breakfast. The poem magnets on the door, a spur to the group's creativity, had been arranged into the inevitable William Carlos Williams poem about eating someone else's plums and not really feeling that bad about it.

Quickly I made some toast, boiled a kettle and thought I had got away without any interaction until I heard someone call cheerfully, 'So that's where the cafetière went!' as I hurried to the staircase with my tray. 'Plenty more in the cupboard by the sink!' I called back. When I reached the top, I found Tom, with his jacket on and the paperback stuffed in a pocket, all ready to go out and engage with nature. It was a good look, I thought enviously. None of my jackets had pockets that could easily accommodate a paperback. I worried that pockets made me look fat. Perhaps this was one of the reasons some men thought women could never be serious writers: we prioritized looks over reading. You did still meet men, sometimes, who claimed never to read books by women, though these days the confession might come accompanied by a mild apology, as though these men regretted the omission but couldn't seriously be expected to correct it.

'Hello, are you off out?' I said.

'I'm going to have a quick walk. All set for this morning?'

'Yes, I think so. Just going to look over my notes while I have breakfast.' My own idea of a morning run was fast retreating. 'Make sure you come back, though! Don't start writing poems somewhere bucolic and lose all track of time.'

'Ha-ha – I won't.'

Two hours later we were well into our first workshop, on 'Sense of Place'. Tom had read aloud a Seamus Heaney poem, 'Blackberry Picking', and was talking about landscape as a source of allegory, as well as political and social commentary. The challenge was to find fresh ways to describe nature, he said, to see its potential for secrets, for clues.

Now he was standing at a flip chart writing a list of nature writing clichés that we were composing together as a group:

snowy peaks
windswept moors
as far as the eye can see
nestling in a valley
cerulean skies
azure sea

'What about rolling hills?' said Kisi.
'Limpid pools,' said Diana.
'Anything majestic,' I offered.
'Sweeping vista,' said Peter.
This was going well. It was good to have Tom there. I never felt comfortable taking the lead or being the focus of attention. I could feel as though I were melting under the hot gaze of expectant faces. As the youngest of three children, I had grown up being stuck in the back, or squeezed in the middle, and was happy with that. On

some car journeys I would even be relegated to the boot, staring out of the rear window at the drivers behind us, too nervous either to smile or stick out my tongue, which was the behaviour normally expected of children travelling in boots back then. Our dog ought to have been in there, but he preferred a seat.

'Any more nature clichés?' Tom tapped the marker pen against his teeth. The night before he had told me about a sixth-form group he recently taught who kept writing his name with love hearts on their palms so that when they put their hands up to answer a question he would see. People on writing courses probably assumed poets were always up for it. 'The resident poet feels duty bound to fondle the freshmen,' says Katherine Dunn in her story about a lecherous writing tutor. Not Tom, though. In fact he told me that adultery was the only thing he hated about Ted Hughes.

A few people looked thoughtfully out of the window at the abundant nature beyond it. Some trees, catching a breeze, obligingly waved back. We probably all felt that nature writing, however fashionable, was too much of an effort. How should you approach it? Should you wander about in it, like Wordsworth or the Brontës? Dig in it, get your hands dirty like Seamus Heaney? Should you train a goshawk, like Helen Macdonald, and run with it bloodied and muddied, tearing through thorn bushes, your sanity on a knife edge? Getting close to nature meant leaving the house in bad weather or when you might not feel like it. One aspiring writer I knew was sent to a forest to get ideas for a poem and opted to watch a video about forests instead. Even Heaney, according to his son Michael, 'wasn't especially fond of the outdoors.'

I remembered my friend's complaint about the mournful sheep. Having lived on a farm as a child, I could agree that sheep and cows, while elusive, weren't complex. You didn't often ask yourself what they were thinking about, because it seemed likely that they weren't thinking very much. This grass here or that grass there was probably the limit of it. That said, for a time we had three sheep – Faith, Hope and Charity. They belonged to someone else, I seemed to remember, and were tenants in the small paddock behind our house. They used to run to greet me when I came home from school, quite unsheeplike – more like dogs really – and let me cuddle them, and I was grateful for the affection, since I was having a bad time with girls in my class. Most sheep are nervy, anxious creatures, but these three seemed to have a bit more about them. More cojones, you might say, although in fact they were ewes.

'Do you want to add anything here?' said Tom, and I realized with a start that I had drifted off. My own notes, now that I hurriedly consulted them, were about how landscape can usefully draw the eye away from some other aspect of the narrative in order to return to it later. How these changes of focus can either be subtly incorporated or dropped in without ceremony. Narrative should not all be on one plane, I said, the picture needs different depths. I gave the example of Mark Twain who, travelling through the Rockies, remembered dropping a watermelon on a friend's head at school.

'There doesn't have to be a reason to make that connection,' I said. 'The watermelon anecdote tells us nothing about the Rockies, except that there is another life beyond what's happening right now. The rest of the world doesn't disappear while you stare at a glacier. Your memories can impose at any moment. You may even reveal the landscape more effectively if you let the reader be drawn away by something unconnected to it. Plus, the anecdote lets Twain find something funny to say in a passage about the Rockies, which aren't otherwise a bag of laughs.'

'Why should they be a bag of laughs?' Peter asked tetchily.

Peter had already complained various times that morning about his uncomfortable chair or our failure to enunciate properly and, like a naughty child, been moved to sit closer to the teachers. Best to treat this as a rhetorical question and move on.

The next exercise required scissors. Everyone had been given a sheet of paper from which I asked them to cut out an oblong.

'The idea is to cut a shape out of the paper big enough to look through, like a viewfinder,' I said, hovering nervously behind the students as they embarked on this project.

A few minutes later the scissors were only half way round the table. Why did things that were supposed to be easy so often become complicated? There was consternation among people who thought they may have made their oblong too big or too small and asked for exact dimensions. One or two of them requested another sheet of paper so that they could make a fresh start. Somebody had to be sent to the office to ask for Sellotape.

'I didn't realize this would take so long', I said to Tom, who was chewing a hangnail.

When all the viewfinders were made, we instructed the writers to get into pairs and denominate themselves either A or B then to follow us out into the garden.

Sheena was anxious about uneven ground. The head injury sustained from her attacker had left her with some difficulties in walking and balance.

'You can stay close to the house, on the paved area. Hang on to me, if you like.'

Teaching often meant lending an arm, bringing a cup of coffee, finding pens and paper. On this week's course I was the fire officer and had been given a high-vis vest and a torch, in case of emergencies at night. My experience as a creative writing teacher seemed far from that of David Foster Wallace, who might spontaneously do a set of squats in the middle of a class at Syracuse University. Sometimes he arrived drinking a Pepsi. 'Excuse me, I'm about to burp,' he would tell the admiring students.

Everyone shuffled outside, where I instructed the As to close their eyes and let the Bs guide them to a part of the garden. Peter and Sheena, being the least mobile, stayed close to the house while Zoe pushed Kisi into a blind gallop towards the fields. Sam had found himself partnered with Lynn, who seemed nervous of touching his bare shoulders. He was wearing the same kind of vest top that had carried him round South Asia and had one of those tattoos that look spiritual but could just as easily be an offensive joke on the part of the tattooist, something that only makes sense to Tamil speakers.

'It takes a leap of faith to let yourself be helpless,' Diana observed.

When all the As had been manoeuvred into position, I asked them to contemplate some small section of the landscape through their viewfinder, creating a mental snapshot they could then go back inside to write about. The As had chosen the view, but the Bs could describe it as they wished so long as they applied originality. Then the exercise was repeated, with Bs directing As.

'Can we take a picture on our phones?' someone asked.

'Obviously not,' said Tom. 'That would be missing the point.'

'Everybody ready?' I clapped my hands together like a primary school teacher. 'You have ten minutes to write your paragraph now, plus fifteen for a coffee.'

Most of the group immediately made for the kettles. Coffee was the corollary to everything on a writing course. We got through gallons of it in a usual week, although a health-conscious contingent increasingly opted for green tea. The others found places to sit, around the communal table in the dining room, in the sitting room, or in the snug, between those two larger rooms and began thoughtfully to apply themselves to this first writing task of the week.

'Remember, we're looking for cliché-free writing!' I said, gathering up my things and walking out of the main room towards the kitchen.

'No clichés!' I called, as I passed the snug.

'Avoid clichés like the plague!' I instructed a small group gathered in the sitting room. In the kitchen three kettles were boiling and packets of biscuits were being torn open. Jules and Jim were making toast with the gusto of lovers who had been too busy in bed to eat at breakfast time. I entered the kitchen triumphantly and someone passed me a coffee. But by the time I had sat down with my coffee in the sun, self-doubt was setting in.

'Maybe clichés aren't such a big deal after all,' I said to Tom.

'Why the change of heart?'

'Because people should write what comes naturally. If you find a deer in the wild majestic, why not say so? It's better than tying yourself in knots trying to be the first person who ever said something clever about a deer. What's wrong with "majestic"?'

'Lazy, I guess,' said Tom, who was rolling a cigarette. 'Does it add anything? Hemingway says you should distrust adjectives the way you distrust certain people.'

'OK. So no adjective at all? That leaves us with "I saw a deer".'

'Yup. I saw a deer. Good, honest, simple writing.'

'Three adjectives right there, mate. Can you roll me one?'

'Sure.' Tom leaned confidentially towards me. 'Word on the street, by the way . . .'

'Yes?'

'Diana's a spy.'

'Shit – what have I been saying?'

'No, she's not spying on us. She was a spy, apparently. MI6. '

'Who told you this?'

'It's Peter's theory.'

'His theory, OK . . .'

'He was talking to her last night. He thinks she's too clever for some of the diplomatic roles she's had. He says she should have got further than first secretary at the British Embassy in Cairo. He worked in Brussels, so I suppose he recognizes the type.'

'Why does all the good stuff happen late at night? When did he tell you, then?'

'I ran into him this morning when I went for a walk.'

'He kept you from your poetry.'

'Luckily poetry's not a finite resource. Plenty more out there.'

'Phew. Thank God.'

'Fuck off.'

'So what did Peter do in Brussels?'

'Some kind of Eurocrat. Trade, I think.'

In another part of the garden we could see Zoe and Kisi talking to Sam. Zoe, in a long flowery dress and Doc

Martens, rocked between her front and back foot while Kisi, in a vintage leather jacket, leaned against a low wall giggling at something. I scanned the garden for Lily, the young insurance broker, and found her sitting on another bench on her own, looking at her phone. Phones were banned at the house in theory and useless in practice as there was no signal. She might be using it as a prop to disguise her loneliness, though, and it gave me a pang to see her sitting there alone. The group dynamics on a writing course often made me think of school, and I may have been oversensitive to the possibility of someone being excluded. These were adults after all. Perhaps they preferred their solitude. They may have come here to get away from other people. All the same, it was interesting, and poignant, to see how everyone arrived on the first day ready to reinvent themselves and how, by midweek, all the original character traits were reasserted, for better or worse. People settled into groups – the popular ones, the quiet ones, the odd troublemaker or outsider.

I slid my shoulder against Tom's and said quietly: 'Who's going to end up with Sam – Zoe or Kisi?'

'Neither. Zoe and Kisi are together.'

'You reckon?'

'Hundred per cent.'

After twenty-five minutes everyone returned to the table. Some of them had produced pages of script, despite an instruction to write no more than two hundred words each. Aspiring writers often seemed contemptuous of word counts, perhaps feeling that no limit should be placed on creativity. But shape and rigour are important too. Letting it all 'flow out' can take you a long way in the wrong direction and make for some tedious writing. Too much freedom could be a bad thing, I thought. A novel should be like a small South American dictatorship – colourful, but rigorously kept in check.

As we settled down, ready to hear the nature pieces read aloud, I became aware of a ripple of alarm moving like a Mexican wave around the table. A folder was being passed from person to person. Everyone who received it, was transformed. Each face switched so quickly from curiosity to horror that the next person was prompted to look over and immediately became horrified in their turn.

'Are we ready to start?' Tom asked.

'Oh my God,' said Lynn, the HR manager.

'That's horrendous,' said Susie, the quiet woman who had said last night that she wanted to be pushed out of her comfort zone. She seemed to be out of it now.

'Fuck sake,' said Sam, blenching.

When the folder reached us, at the top of the table, I couldn't at first decipher the photos which seemed to show two views of a sponge pudding, liberally doused with strawberry jam. Then Sheena, sitting beside me, leaned over and spoke in a confidential tone, tapping the photos with a manicured nail.

'That's where my neighbour got me with the sword.'

'Jesus Christ!'

'That's from the top and that's from the back. See? I wanted to get some feedback from the group about whether to include them in my pitch to the publisher.'

'OK, we'll have a think. It's awful – I mean what happened to you.' I quickly passed the folder back to Sheena.

'I know. And all over a leylandii.'

We listened to the group read their nature pieces. Nick had compared the hills he saw through his viewfinder to breasts and there was some discussion over whether that was a cliché or wrong in a different way since there were three hills. Lynn had simply described what she saw: long grass, dark hills, blue sky, white clouds and so on.

'Great – it's like a kind of list poem!' said Tom brightly and Lynn blushed at this new understanding of herself as a poet.

'Now time for today's homework.' There was groaning as the students reverted to their school days and the pleasure of responding collectively to some perceived injustice.

Tom had devised an exercise connected to our theme based on the five senses. 'We want you to travel back to some point in your life and evoke the feeling of that time. Concentrate on all the senses. Don't just tell us what you saw, but what you smelled, heard, touched and tasted. So, if you're writing about a café, we want to feel the sticky Formica, smell the frying bacon. Not more than five hundred words, please.'

'Does it have to be a real place?' asked Susie, looking worried.

'No,' said Tom. 'But you'll probably find that you draw on a real place even if you describe an imaginary one.'

'Do we have to do this if we have other writing to be getting on with?' asked Lynn, face slumped in her hands. There was always somebody who didn't want to do the exercise.

'You never have to do anything if you don't want to. Oh, and everyone remember to sign up for the one-to-one sessions this afternoon.'

'And if you want us to read anything before meeting this afternoon, bring it now,' I added.

After lunch I walked up the road to the top of hill then sat on a bench looking out over the valley. This might be the only opportunity in the day for fresh air and I took a few deep gulps, filling my lungs as we are told to do in childhood, as though oxygen had some moral benefit, then looked around me, trying to cram every beautiful thing in through my eyes in the time available, filling a well I could draw on later. The writing week could be intense and cloistered. The scenery was glorious, but mostly we saw it through glass.

These days I longed for nature with the same unfocussed desire I had felt for the city as a teenager. It wasn't that I didn't know, back then, that I was lucky to live somewhere beautiful. Whenever I left the family farm, to go to London, for example, it was always a relief to get back home. But I was lonely on the farm, and had no friends living nearby. Sometimes I'd climb through a small window in the attic, out onto the roof of our house and look over the countryside for miles around, barely another house in sight, already nostalgic for the moment that I knew was coming when I would miss this view – missing it in advance, almost – even if I could scarcely enjoy it at the time. And now I had become one of the city-dwellers I used to despise, one of those people who got very impressed by trees, who gasped over a single wildflower in the hedgerow, who looked to nature for life lessons, as though it had been arranged as an allegory for people like me.

We wanted nature as an antidote to our human mis-takes when in fact so many parts of our little country had been shaped by human hands, the wilderness we could see reinserted in areas of defunct industry. The slag heaps my mother grew up among in Yorkshire had been covered over and turned into hills. Did it matter, so long as they looked pretty? For the poet and essayist Kathleen Jamie, 'wild' is a word like 'soul'. 'Such a thing may not exist, but we want it, and we know what we mean when we talk about it.'

The person who wrote about the 'mournful gaze of a sheep' probably didn't know what it felt like to grab a sheep by its scruff, feeling that wedge of muscle and wool in your grip, as you thrust it towards the dipping pen. They couldn't imagine the stout warmth of the body held between a shearer's legs, the winter coat falling away in heavy folds to leave a body etched with lines. Sylvia Plath herself wrote a poem about sheep but she, not the sheep, was the mournful presence in it.

I could see Peter walking steadily up the hill from the house, the bald patch on his head glinting as he moved between patches of shadow and sun. With every step he planted his walking stick in the manner of someone who would not suffer fools gladly, as though he knew this was something people said about him and didn't shrink from the aspersion. It must be tiring to be propelled through life by irritation, but perhaps it made for a steady fuel. As he got closer it became clear that Peter was aiming for me and that I, on this occasion, was the insufferable fool.

'Hello Peter,' I said, moving along the bench. He eased himself down onto it with a smell of well-worn tweed that faintly evoked the wet fleece of a sheep. 'I hope you enjoyed this morning's workshop?'

'Well yes,' he said with a chuckle that sounded as though it had been selected from a range of chuckles, each conveying a marginally different degree of condescension. 'Although it was perhaps not strictly relevant to my own writing.'

'I don't know about that. All of it should be relevant in some way, shouldn't it? Even if it just sparks an idea?'

'I've been reading your book about Spain.'

'Oh, that's very kind of –'

'I'm afraid it's riddled with errors.'

'Really?' Riddled, I thought. He was going in hard. Peter sat back, his stringy thighs braced against the wooden slats.

'For example you've written "treaty" where you meant "treatise". A translating error, no doubt, from the Spanish "*tratado*".'

I knew immediately that he was right: I had made that mistake.

'So I'd like to make you an offer. I will compile a list of the errors in your book if you arrange a meeting between myself and your agent to take place in the next few months.'

'Wow. Really?'

Peter's face settled into the arrangement of ridges and furrows in which his pained certainty had found expression over many decades. I wondered briefly if a comparison could be made between his undulating forehead and the hilly landscape and decided that was too much of a stretch. Peter's forehead was not like Yorkshire.

'It's a fair exchange. I'll be saving you a lot of work.'

'You could say that if a reader finds mistakes in someone's book, the honourable thing to do is to let the author know without expecting anything in return.'

'Ah, well maybe I'm not very honourable.'

'To be honest it sounds like blackmail!'

'Not at all,' Peter said, with a tight smile that I could imagine had been proffered across many conference tables in Brussels.

'I'm not sure that's the kind of arrangement I want to enter into, anyway. I don't think my agent would be comfortable with it.'

'Very well. Let me know if you change your mind.' He

shuffled forward on the bench and needed several movements to swing onto his feet. I resisted the temptation
to help.

So my book was riddled with errors. I looked across the
valley, hills and trees, trees and hills, as far as the eye could
see, and found no particular solace there.

Exercise One

A Sense of Place

When I was ten years old my parents moved to a farm in Sussex and sent me to a small school that smelled of polished wood, urine and mashed potato. A craze for instant mash was sweeping the country that year, sparked by some TV adverts in which visiting aliens laughed at Earthlings for bothering to boil and mash up real potatoes. It was the 1970s and we were enchanted by the capacity of flattened foodstuffs to acquire another dimension. To watch the components of a Minestrone – desiccated carrot, potato and green beans – come to life in a mug was as much excitement as anyone needed at lunchtime. Packet food was intergenerational, combining a nostalgia for wartime rations with the thrill of space travel. With the simple addition of water, whole meals sprang out of a box. At home we sometimes assembled chow mein or cheesecake from a series of packets. My friends and I made Angel Delight from a packet too, or just ate it straight from the foil envelope with a spoon, choking down the dust or blowing clouds of it into each others' faces. This was the modern way to eat and ours felt like a golden age of time-saving process and devices. 'Soon,' my mother said, 'we'll all eat pills instead of meals.'

At school instant mash accompanied every meal and was compulsory, along with more traditional offerings such as Spotted Dick or crumble. Puddings came with lumpy custard and were meant to be a challenge because being British meant never fully surrendering to pleasure. This was the bolstering stodge that had propelled earlier generations off to distant corners of the empire, perhaps in search of better food. The cooks were unhappy making it and we were unhappy eating it, but doing something you did not like was a good way to build character. Meanwhile, any attempt to avoid food risked a reference to the starving poor because our school, and others like it, was involved in a bold experiment to correct the injustice of malnutrition in parts of Africa by over-feeding children at home. I carried a signed note from home letting me off pudding and other girls had notes letting them off Games, but all our notes were dismissed as a contemptible display of weakness. Once I produced mine in protest at a jam roly-poly and the teacher shouted at me in front of everyone. I was like Oliver Twist, only asking for less, and nobody sang.

For two hundred years Kent and Sussex had been the heartland of British beer production, but now many of the oasthouses once used for drying and storing hops had been converted, this small country school among them. Our classroom, one of the three oasts, was round, and that was unfortunate because it meant that there were no corners to hide in. I was much the youngest of the ten girls in my class and – for reasons I didn't fully understand – unpopular with at least half of them. The girls had all known each other since they started aged four or five and didn't welcome a newcomer.

This low status was painful because at my previous school I had been one of the popular ones, right at the top of the playground hierarchy. I used to choose which games we played at break, keeping the best roles for myself, and lead delegations from the girls' corner of the playground to the boys' whenever an invitation came – and they came most lunchtimes – to look down someone's pants. A boy called Neil was always keen to show us his penis and we were usually curious enough to oblige, although none of us wanted anyone looking down our own pants. We must have known already that the rules were different for boys and girls; we had to protect our tender reputations. Regular games of Kiss Chase encouraged the view that men were hunters and women needed to be fit to keep ahead. I sometimes slowed down enough to let myself be kissed by a boy called Clive, who had taught me how to do up my shoelaces – an act of kindness I never forgot. There was a happy atmosphere of mischief at this school. The boys were proud to be seen waiting in the line for the headmaster's office to be caned after lunch (only one girl ever got caned and that was for setting fire to the changing rooms). On my last day at that school I spotted Neil standing in the caning queue and called out 'See you never!' He grinned and shouted back 'Have a good life!'

But I wasn't having a good life, not in Sussex. The new school was girls only, and all the rules seemed to be different, especially the unspoken ones. I wore a dress to the summer barbecue and was haughtily informed that only jeans were cool. People looked slyly in my direction as they circulated notes in class. They hid my clothes in the changing room. Within weeks of arriving I got 'sent to Coventry', for no reason I could pinpoint other than being new. One girl appeared to be leading the bullying campaign and years later I discovered that she had been unhappy and dealing with difficult family circumstances. In retrospect these things make sense, but at the time I hated her and I hated school. Even the two girls who still spoke to me were frightening: at break Belinda made me play a violent game called 'Horses'; I had to cling to her back while she cantered around the hard court trying to throw me off. Penny used to bring an album of pornographic pictures to school and show them to us as we sat on the grass, making daisy chains under a chestnut tree in the garden. The grainy pictures of men and women, though hard to decipher, were troubling in a way that made Neil's exposure in the boy's corner seem innocent. What were they doing? Whichever way we turned the pictures, none of us could make it out. I never found out how Penny got hold of this explicit material, but I did once spend a weekend with her family and remember that everyone got up early to go to Mass.

I started dreading school and became introverted at home.

'Join a club!' my mother urged, but I was nervous of the Brownies – they might all be like the girls at school – and too anxious to try out tennis. The Young Ornithologists cancelled my membership when I failed to sign up for any expeditions; I wasn't all that interested in birds. How life had changed. Back at my old school I had never expected to be unpopular, and now I could barely imagine ever being popular again.

Perhaps I didn't know how to get on with other children, for home was a grown-up world. By the time I was twelve, my brother and sister were in their twenties and lived away, first at university then in London, where they worked. Every few weeks they would come home trailing cigarette smoke, casually swearing and starting arguments about politics. My sister, who worked in advertising, might bring a copy of *Vogue* which I could look at if I washed my hands first. She smelled of expensive perfume and something indeterminate, a kind of sooty glamour, the smell of London as imagined in old black and white films. My brother was skinny and very clever and these two attributes seemed to be connected, as if all the thinking was burning up calories faster than he could replace them. There were ten years between him and me and that gap, too big for sibling tensions or rivalry, became instead a place for indulgence. Richard could seem more like a doting uncle than a brother, arranging tickling sessions and treasure hunts, arriving on my birthday with joke books or a magic set. He helped me learn how to read and patiently demystified the 24-hour clock, which had come as a shocking revelation to me, like discovering that every day contained a hidden dimension. How could it ever be 17 o'clock? Later, when I went to stay with him in London as a teenager, he let me tag along to meet his friends in pubs or scruffy flat shares, apparently unembarrassed by my punkish experiments with make-up and army surplus. By then I knew that my brother was suffering from depression. He had trouble holding down jobs, seemed to get into arguments with his bosses and was increasingly despondent about his options. On a busy train I noticed him block his ears against the clamour of slamming doors. At home, his visits were a source of tension – whenever he came back the household seemed to brace itself for conflict. I knew that there were rows after I had gone to bed or was out of the way, but I didn't really know what they were about.

My parents hadn't 'expected' me, their much younger child and, although they made me welcome, there was also a feeling that I had never been part of the plan. It was years before I realized how useful that detachment was, especially for a writer. It must be enjoyable to be at the centre of attention, but the unplanned child is free to come and go without anyone noticing, to skirt the action and see what's going on without the responsibility of taking part. Occasionally I walked into rooms that were heavy with aftermath. Somebody would be sweeping up broken china; someone would be sitting alone, head in hands. Two people might break off a conversation. 'Once again I am not wanted', I wrote petulantly in my diary. The air contained a mystery it probably wasn't my place to ask about, so I took myself off, spending hours hitting a tennis ball against a wall outside or riding around the farm on my bike. I would cycle to the river, to watch voles dip in and out of the riverbank, or to a hidden glade, where I imagined long stories about woodland creatures. I organized the reference cards sent by the Young Ornithologists into a file or played in the barn, climbing to the top of the straw stack and moving bales around to make a big living area like the one the Beatles inhabited in *Help!* I sat on the bales and imagined that one of the Beatles, or all of them, was singing me a love song.

Keeping insects in a jar, playing in rivers, lazing in wheat fields: these are the pastimes that city dwellers think constitute an idyllic upbringing. I did those things and, looking back, it seems idyllic even to me. At the time, though, I was lonely and worried about school, and my life seemed boring, especially compared with my American pen pal's. Julie sent regular missives from New York, where her father worked as a lawyer in the Bronx.

Hi Panda, how are you?! Everyone in my family is alright and I hope everyone in your family is alright too. Yesterday I was with Dad in his office when someone fired through the window!!! We had to hide under the desk!!! It was SOOOO scary!!! In America the televisions have 7 channels. How many does the English one have? I am going to get a huge poster of Andy Gibb. Hope you like these Snoopy stickers!!!

The holidays hung heavy and Sundays were cumbersome: the soul beaten into submission by church in the morning, and the body following it after a roast dinner that took hours to digest. Disapproving of the vicar, my father sat through sermons with a stony expression. 'For these and all his mercies, the Lord's name be praised,' he said, before we sat down to eat beef that was difficult to cut and then difficult to chew. Then we chewed over the sermon.

While my school didn't offer much in the way of science (it was hard to get the teachers), there was great enthusiasm for literature. Between the ages of ten and twelve our class tackled Hardy, Dickens, a Brontë and several Shakespeares. Josephine Tey's *The Daughter of Time*, about Richard III and the princes in the tower, introduced us to the idea that fiction, though invented, could help set the historical record straight; a lie could be truthful. We learned poems and stood grouped in one half of the circular classroom, chanting them at the headmistress, who sat in the other.

Then during a class called Nature, we followed Miss S., an elderly lady in slacks, around the garden, looking at bees and butterflies. Our English lessons roamed over five centuries of literature and criticism, but the furthest reach of scientific enquiry in our Nature class was when Miss S. plucked the head off a flower and dissected it to show us the stamen.

Latin was also on the syllabus but I arrived not having studied any. So once a week, in an arrangement that apparently raised no eyebrows, the headmistress's husband, 'Sir', took me up to their bedroom for extra Latin. We sat at the foot of the marital bed, looking out over the garden, where Miss S. may have been inducting a new generation into the wonders of pollination, while Sir tested me on vocabulary and verb forms. The tests weren't rigorous because it wasn't in Sir's nature to put others to trial. His default mode was sunny, and he often seemed lost in a dream. He walked beaming around the school and grounds, came beaming through the dining room at lunchtime, where everyone else was miserably eating mashed potato. Sir preferred to get me interested in Latin by reading me passages from Pliny and involving me in the mystery of their deciphering. Once, he was so keen to show me what a toga looked like that he pulled the quilt and blankets off the carefully made bed, whipped off the sheet and draped it around himself. I had never seen an adult do something so thrillingly transgressive. Sir's rebellious act helped me fall in love with Latin and I began to wish ardently to have been a Roman.

After school I waited with the others at the door, longing for my mother to come, anxious that she wouldn't, then flooded with relief when her car turned in to the school gate, a fringe of flowery material flapping from the driver's door like the flag of a rescue party because she tended to catch her dress in the door as she closed it, and sometimes drove off with her handbag on the roof, too. Our dog Gulliver was often beside her in the passenger seat with his tongue lolling out. One afternoon as we drove away from school, I told her about being bullied and saw her frowning in the rear-view mirror: I had given her another thing to worry about. She offered to speak to the headmistress and of course I said no. Sitting in the back of our new Simca, my bare legs squeaking on the plastic coverings, I looked at my mother and Gulliver, and felt that neither of them cared all that much.

My parents thought it was important for children to be 'toughened up'. They themselves had grown up during the war, survived bacterial infections in the pre-antibiotic age and been discouraged from great displays of emotion. My mother rarely mentioned the brother who had been killed in action at the age of nineteen and I decided, with the selfish logic of a child, that it must be because we, her real family, meant so much more to her than the family in which she had grown up. Every child must think some variation on this: that the parent's childhood home was merely a rehearsal for *this*, the genuine family experience. Each generation of parents becomes a framing device for their children's story.

That wartime stoicism was conveyed in various ways at home, including a delight in tinned food, a lack of central heating and a preference for medicated toilet paper with zero absorbency. You had to be quick, or the urine slid off it onto your hand. This was not only a test of wits but proof of frugality and higher mindedness; soft toilet paper, like ITV, was for weaker characters. Our ancient farmhouse rustled with life: mice and woodworm – which left mounds of sawdust under the furniture – and deathwatch beetle, which could be heard tapping in the rafters at night. In the winter months long strips of ice laced our windows. I piled my school clothes up beside the bed so that I could put them on in the morning under the covers, wriggling into my woollen tights in a horizontal dance. If it was too cold for the car to start I'd have to push it out of the garage, my mother pulling on the choke, then chase her down the hill, while the engine jump-started, before catching up at the bottom. The summer was a different story: Gulliver liked to travel with his whole head out of the window, ears and tongue flapping, grinning at other road-users. Perhaps all dogs in cars have something of the Californian babe about them on sunny days.

By the age of twelve I was bad at Maths and Science, average at History and Geography and, thanks to Sir and his wife, good at Latin and English. On this slim recommendation I went off to Roedean, a boarding school in Brighton. My parents, though frugal in many respects, thought that boarding schools were the best way to foster independence in children and toughen them up and that this process should start as early as possible. My brother had been sent away aged eight. I was lucky to have clung to the mothership four years longer. I didn't see the place that was going to be my home for the next five years until the day I arrived there with a trunk full of new uniform ready for the winter term. In my memory we rounded a corner and gasped in unison as the building loomed above us, a grey stone fortress perched on a cliff-top. The school had been founded in 1885 by Penelope, Dorothy and Millicent Lawrence, three doughty sisters whose aim – radical at the time – was to prepare girls for university, not merely for marriage. By 1898 they had needed bigger premises, and the choice of this wind-blasted site and Gothic architecture can't have been accidental. Roedean seemed to have been built to intimidate all comers, whether they approached by land, sea or sky.

Going away to school was exciting, all the same. For the first time ever I slept with a duvet and lost it almost nightly off the top bunk. I had friends with the kind of names you find in boarding school romps – Bunny, Squeaky and Podge. Some of the other new girls had read Malory Towers and arrived eager for the boarding school experience, with tuck boxes and gym knickers. In fact all of us had been told to bring two pairs of gym knickers, although we never wore them. Their purpose must have been more symbolic than practical, a reminder that there was nothing sexy about the pelvic region.

It was a surprise, and a relief, to find myself back in the popular set at this school; I happened to have been assigned to the popular girls' dormitory and they liked me. In time I became, if not one the coolest girls at school, then in the next rank down – about three-quarters cool. In lessons I sat in the third row, not the back: bold enough to smirk at the antics of the fourth row, but not to join in. I wasn't cool enough to pretend to be injecting heroin with my retractable pencil, like the girls in the back row. I wasn't as cool as the girls who wore make-up and dangly earrings in defiance of the rules. I was cool enough to roll my skirt up above the knee, but not as far as the thigh. I was cool enough to smoke with some other girls in the bathroom at night, but not cool enough to avoid crying when we got caught and told we couldn't go home for the rest of term.

In this strange and rarified world friends counted for much more than adults, who seemed tangential to our lives and mostly absent from them once the school day was over. Whether it was designed to lock us in or to lock out those who might distract us from our studies, our chilly stronghold did not itself seem to us a source of security. We made each other feel safe.

After 'lights out', we hurried down the corridors in our pyjamas to the rooms of older girls who handed out cigarettes and told stories of sexual encounters that included codes and acronyms we struggled to decipher back in our own rooms. At night the darkened downstairs corridors filled with cockroaches. We huddled up in our dormitories, hoping that cockroaches couldn't climb stairs. Occasionally we arranged midnight feasts but they were never as much fun as they seemed in Malory Towers. If it was stormy, the sea crashed against the cliffs and the foghorn sounded every thirty seconds. We shone our torches out of the window, looking for men, as a joke, although some did occasionally penetrate the grounds, and one or two of the girls. The rest of us quietly guarded our virginity. My best friend and I had resolved to keep it until after we left school – the easiest option, in fact, since it would be logistically difficult to lose it any earlier. Parading in our regulation cloaks in front of the mock Gothic facade on windswept days, we may have looked like the French Lieutenant's Woman pining for our men at sea, when any kind of lover would have done. A few girls had their first sexual encounters right there, on the stony beach below the cliffs.

My brother and sister came to visit me at school one summer and caused a sensation by smoking and swearing in the common room and by their good looks and stylish clothes. I sat with them, smoke curling around me, and noticed with satisfaction how every few minutes the door would crack open and a new bunch of girls would peer admiringly round it, including one or two prefects. This was going to be excellent for my reputation. One of the girls, Podge most likely, formed an instant crush on my brother so I let her borrow a photograph of him and she stuck it on her wall next to a poster of David Bowie.

One evening as I was talking to a friend about various

teenage grievances, the door flew open and our house mistress fell into the room like an eavesdropping butler in a French farce.

'How dare you expose yourselves!' she cried, although both of us were swaddled in woollen tights, jumpers, scarves, fingerless gloves and leg warmers. It was extremely cold.

Later that evening I was summoned to the house mistress's flat.

'You think that people like you, but they don't,' said Mrs T. 'They just want to use you.'

My house mistress, who appeared to be drunk, then embarked on a tirade that seemed to go on for hours. I was a failure, she said, and not clever enough to be wasting time on unsuitable friendships. My attention wandered to the shoes she had confiscated from me the previous term because the heels were more than the regulation inch high. For a long time they had been visible on the other side of the glass door to her flat; I would see them every time I went up and down the stairs between our bedrooms and the front hall, but now they had disappeared. I wondered what had happened to them and if I would ever get them back. I wondered what the people who didn't really like me might be using me for. There was no obvious answer to either question.

'Every single one of your teachers has complained about your attitude and your standard of work,' said Mrs T., mid-harangue, inadvertently pushing her campaign too far: I didn't believe her, and the next day, when I asked my form teacher, she confirmed my suspicions. Nobody had complained. I didn't tell my parents about the unsettling experience and so nothing was done about the housemistress, who might have claimed to be building character. That, after all, was the goal of a public-school education, whether achieved through discipline, sports or challenging food. The episode was revealing though; it showed that adults could lie, and that seemed like an interesting sign of weakness.

All things considered, at the age of fifteen my life wasn't too bad. Three-quarters cool and with my O-levels out of the way, I was best friends with the most popular girl in my year. At a party during the summer half-term break I had acquired a boyfriend who gave me a love bite, briefly making me famous at school. I was going to have to retake Maths O-level – twice, in fact – but otherwise life was looking all right.

On an August afternoon in 1982 I was sitting in my room at home writing a letter to a friend when I heard my parents coming towards the door. They knocked, came in and both put their arms around me. My father said that there had been a terrible accident: my brother had fallen from a building. It was an odd way to describe an accident. I waited for more information. What had he hurt, where was he now and when were we going to visit him? But no more was said and it was in the absence of words that I understood. My father left the room and my mother asked

41

me if I would like a cup of tea, that universal remedy, sweetened when it is for shock. She sat beside me and held my hand but I needed to move. I left the room and ran downstairs and outside, off down the hill to the river at the bottom of our farm. Looking back towards the house I could see that a police car was parked outside it, a physical confirmation of something serious, of terrible news being broken. The confirmations seemed necessary because the information on its own was hard to absorb. Later my father spoke of his sympathy for the young police officers who had had to inform him of my brother's death.

That long day, the last day of my childhood, was marked by shock, by vivid impressions. My sister was sent home from work, sixty miles in a London taxi, an expensive gesture that – like the police car – gave weight to the idea that something really awful must have happened. My father worried that Richard's death might be on the news and my sister reassured him, with remarkable composure, that 'he won't have been the only one today.' That may have been the moment I realized my brother had killed himself. Nobody had told me he had, but there had been the oddness of the phrase 'he's fallen from a building', and now this observation of my sister's.

It was only the next day that grief moved in and began its heavy progression through the body to the heart. We often talk about heartache as though it were a metaphor, but grief really does hurt in the chest cavity, something to do with stress hormones constricting the arteries. To doctors, a broken heart is 'stress cardiomyopathy'. From now on I would wake up every morning and have that experience, familiar to all the newly bereaved, of taking a few seconds to remember that the world had turned upside down.

Two weeks later I was back at school, where one of the first assignments of the term was to write about what happened in the summer holidays, in French. 'But don't write about anything very sad,' said our teacher, Madame C., hovering near my desk with a heavy scent of Opium. 'Nothing about death or anything.' I felt the eyes of the class swivel towards me.

'That was so kind of Madame C.,' said my best friend afterwards, as we walked to lunch. 'She was obviously talking about you.' It was particularly grievous that my best friend had noticed this gesture and misread it as genuinely kind.

'She could just have set a different essay,' I said.

'But we always do "what happened in the summer".'

'She knew what happened in the summer. She could easily have avoided it. She could have set "if I were Prime Minister".'

'She wanted us to practise the *passé composé*,' said my friend, crossly.

The tip of her nose went red whenever she felt indignant about something and I was sad to see this happening on Madame C.'s behalf, rather than mine. My best friend was poised, beautiful and the archetypal boarding-school heroine, captain of every team, top of every class and destined to become Head Girl. Despite eating three or four chocolate bars every day, she had a perfect figure. She was the kind of girl boys you like ask you about, dashing your own hopes. I can't remember how we became best friends – sometimes these arrangements began with an official proposal – 'will you be my best friend?' – sometimes best-friendship developed over time without needing acknowledgement, but she was always loyal to me, picking me for her netball team even when it was bound to damage her side's chances of winning. It was wounding to feel she didn't understand.

I resigned myself to finding something cheerful to say in French about the events of the summer. But Madame C.'s torment didn't end there. It turned out that one of our A-level set books in French was Jean Anouilh's *Antigone*, based on the Greek tragedy by Sophocles. Anouilh's version was first performed in 1944 and Sophocles' 2,300 years earlier. In both versions Antigone is a young woman whose warring brothers Polynices and Etiocles have been killed in battle for the city of Thebes. Their uncle Creon, now King of Thebes, honours Etiocles with a hero's burial, while Polynices is to be left unburied for the vultures to scavenge. Antigone refuses to obey Creon's edict, because leaving a body unburied offends the will of the gods. She vows to bury her brother and to keep burying his body every time it is uncovered. Her punishment is to be walled up alive by Creon, and Antigone kills herself inside this prison.

Few fifteen-year-olds could have felt so strongly a young woman's anguish over an unburied brother. Just two weeks earlier I had sat in my bedroom wondering – but not daring to ask anyone – if Richard could even be buried in consecrated ground, since he had committed suicide. I was fresh from the graveside, still in the grip of that rage, that wild energy that accompanies grief. Not only had I lost my brother but I was ashamed and daunted by the manner of his death. Reading *Antigone* somehow brought home the responsibility of association. The Greek heroine's brother is dead and dishonoured so she kills herself. Was that the way things went? That death impulse and its power to affect other people, perhaps to draw them towards it, was frightening. How much of Richard's tragedy attached to our family and how much was it going to alter our lives? Would we become tragic by association? That was what I feared: difference and isolation.

I had to ask Podge to return the photo she had borrowed.

A violent death throws the world into disorder. That something so awful could happen and that life should go on as before makes no sense. Why should we do all the things we used to do – brush our hair, clean our teeth, meekly obey timetables, make polite conversation at meal times? The responses of Greek tragedy – wailing, rending clothing, vengeful murder – made more sense, even if they weren't workable solutions for me at school. Counselling would have been a quieter option, but in those days it was neither available nor considered particularly helpful: better to move on. My teachers regarded the suicide as a misfortune that I should put behind me in order to concentrate on A-levels and university applications. My house mistress seemed vindicated in her assessment of me as marked for failure. A well-meaning friend assured me that my brother's death could not have been avoided because suicidal people were 'always going to do it.'

One of my mother's friends wrote to assure her that 'children get over things quickly', and I couldn't forgive that casual sidelining of my grief. I would have done anything to have Richard back; I would not 'get over' him. Channelling my energy into school work, I carried my grief around like a grenade. The fury went inwards and eventually subsided. It takes perhaps ten years for grief to lose its raw edge. After that time thinking about my brother was no longer, in itself, a reason to cry. I still felt very sad about the young man who had so much to offer the world and whose life had been cut short, but there was a distance between the person he had been, frozen in time now, and the person I was becoming. The visceral connection had gone. It was sad to lose it, but life must be lived.

That was how things continued, until, thirty years after my brother died, I got a letter from one of his friends.

DAY TWO HANDOUT

Leary was middle-aged now, married, the father of six children. He was a small, wiry man with tight features and bloodshot eyes, his spareness occasionally reminding people of a hedgerow animal they could not readily name. Sparse grey hair was brushed straight back from the narrow dome of his forehead. Two forefingers, thumbs, middle fingers, upper lip and teeth, were stained brown from cigarettes he manufactured with the aid of a small machine. Leary did not wear overalls when at work and was rarely encountered in clothes that did not bear splashes of paint.

from *Widows*, by WILLIAM TREVOR

Grandfather's skirts would flap in the wind along the churchyard path and I would hang on. He often found things to do in the vestry, excuses for getting out of the vicarage (kicking the swollen door, cursing) and so long as he took me he couldn't get up to much. I was a sort of hobble; he was my minder and I was his. He'd have liked to get further away, but petrol was rationed. The church was at least safe. My grandmother never went near it – except feet first in her coffin, but that was years later, when she was buried in the same grave with him. Rotting together for eternity, one flesh at the last after a lifetime's mutual loathing. In life, though she never invaded his patch; once inside the churchyard gate he was on his own ground, in his element. He was good at funerals, being gaunt and lined, marked with mortality. He had a scar down his hollow cheek too, which Grandma had done with the carving knife one of the many times when he came home pissed and incapable.

from *Bad Blood*, by LORNA SAGE

Day Two

Writing School

On the second morning I woke up, wolfed down breakfast in the solitude of my room, looking hungrily out at the trees and hills, then got dressed and put on my trainers. I was going to go for a run. I was going to be the woman who casually fits in a run at the start of a productive working day.

But not before I had washed and returned my cafetière to the kitchen, where there were already small signs of rebellion. 'GOAT'S milk please' was chalked on the blackboard. Some empty wine bottles on the counter were a reminder that there had been laughter coming from the kitchen sometime around midnight. Half asleep, I had tried to identify the voices. Sam and the festival girls, I thought, but it sounded as though someone older was there too. The fridge poem had been subtly rearranged.

I have eaten
the patriarchy
which
you left in the world
and which
you were probably
enjoying
Forgive me
Actually you

The mystery of that unfinished last line detained me for a few seconds as I stretched my calf muscles. 'Patriarchy' had been written in tiny letters on a scrap of paper and inserted into the poem, there being no fridge magnet for that word in this particular set. I unlatched the back door, walked away from the house and, once I was distant enough not to be seen, started running, hopping between tree stumps, wary of turning my ankle, which I had nastily twisted the year before. Soon I came to a fork in the woods and, like the man in Robert Frost's poem, took the less travelled path, then continued up, half running, half walking, towards the brow of the hill, thinking how Frost's poem had been misconstrued as an argument for taking less obvious choices in life, when in fact it had simply been meant as a joke about an indecisive friend. I had read somewhere that

Frost was disappointed when an audience of students failed to find the poem funny, and that his friend, the one who inspired the poem, was disappointed to learn that it was meant to be a joke and not a tribute. So many poems must get taken the wrong way, I thought. So many must cause disappointment, embarrassment or offence. For instance, how did Craig Raine's wife feel about him comparing her breasts to 'tender blisters'? Perhaps she didn't mind. People who slept with poets probably expected their bodies to be used for material. I'd be tempted to strike some kind of bargain though – a meal out for every nipple. City break for a vagina.

On and up I went, through trees that had grown tall in the competition for sunlight, thin and leggy, like rich London girls. At the next junction, I went right again. Borges wrote about paths, too, in 'The Garden of Forking Paths', a story I had read when studying Spanish at university, although that was really about the circular nature of time. Come to think of it, a whole exercise could be planned around forking paths, perhaps even a workshop. It would be a good way to do something different, get everyone out of the house. Sheena and Peter wouldn't be keen, though, and it was probably too late for this week. Here I was, running and planning work at the same time, like some Silicon Valley techpreneur. I carried on up, heart playing a pleasant percussion on my ribcage, before deciding it was time to get back to the house and prepare for that morning's session, which was beginning in an hour. I turned round, and started walking down, gradually catching my breath. In a few minutes I arrived at the first meeting of paths, which looked quite different when approached from this angle. There was no clear path down, but two options, both of which meandered sideways. The one on the right looked a better bet, but could I trust that instinct? My spatial awareness had never been good and now it occurred to me that I was someone who always took the path on the right, which made no sense when trying to retrace your footsteps. Or did it? Should one always veer right, or rather veer right on the way out and left on the way home? Robert Frost hadn't gone into this. I took the left-hand path anyway and half-ran along it for a while before beginning to feel that I ought by now to have come to the second junction. Less than an hour to go until the morning workshop. I could see the house down below me, just couldn't work out how to get to it. This was ridiculous; I started to run. If the junction wasn't round the next corner, then I must have made the wrong choice and would have to return to the last one, to take the other path. I rounded a bend – no junction – and ran on to the next bend – no junction – at which point I turned around and started running back. My heart was thudding now in a way that was no longer pleasant but skirting nausea, although I could still appreciate that it was funny to be lost in the woods a bare mile from the house, running back and forth through the trees, in full sight of my objective, literally acting out the kind of tired metaphor relied on in Gothic novels. The analogies were too rich. The overgrown paths and under-growth – Angela Carter would surely make something sexual of it. Back at the first junction I took the left-hand path, ran for a few minutes crunching sticks underfoot and saw, with great relief, the way that led back to civilization.

Only twenty minutes before the workshop, the kitchen was full of people still making breakfast or clearing it away. I felt like Alice in Wonderland waking up on the river bank. Nobody knew what I had endured. The world was safe, after all, and smelled of toast.

'Have you been for a run, darling?' Jules asked.

'Kind of.'

'Oh bravo!' said Diana, turning back from the sink, as though to praise a small child.

'Somehow I managed to get lost. Not for long but—' No point now trying to look like someone returning from a regular morning run.

'Oh bless!' Jules put her hand on my hair, tucking a loop of it behind my ear. She was tactile in a way that could make you feel tearful for no reason. Yesterday I had found out that she and Jim had only been together a few months, which seemed to explain their ardour. They had met at a swimming pool when she dropped her ring in the water and he dived in to retrieve it.

'Look at that glorious blue sky,' said Jules, standing at the door. Blonde hair streamed sunnily down her back. Every part of her seemed happy with life. 'Perhaps we should do the workshop outside this morning?'

'That's a nice idea – might be tricky for some people, though. I'll confer with Tom. Anyway, I'd better get ready now and just – you know – just—'

Somebody thrust a coffee into my hands. Over-caffeinated they might be, but residential courses were loving too. It was heartening to see how people from different backgrounds and age groups quickly learned to live together, even forming lasting friendships. While lunches were provided by staff at the centre, the participants took it in turn to cook dinner in groups and sometimes arguments broke out in the kitchen, but generally the experiment worked. One group I had taught still kept in touch with each other and me, circulating news of their writing accomplishments and spurring each other on to finish manuscripts or enter competitions. And there were others who went to festivals together or met in pub rooms to listen to each other's work.

I liked living with other people – I'd been at a boarding school, after all – and sometimes wondered what it would be like to live in a commune or a convent. In communes the implicit absence of a power structure must inevitably come to grate, whereas in a convent the authority lines up through mother superior, the bishop and God were indisputable – everyone would know her place. That said, I had a friend for some time who was a nun and when I went to stay with her at the convent, it was clear that there was friction among the sisters; I remember an argument over a missing pot of strawberry jam.

While Jules was someone who saw possibility in everything, Sheena always saw calamity – understandably, given that she had once been attacked from behind with a ceremonial sword. She preferred to keep the workshop indoors and at ten o'clock we reconvened around the table with our coffees and notebooks.

It was my turn to start proceedings. 'Today we're going to talk about character,' I began. My whole body moved to riot whenever I had to speak in public. An exploding heart could be remedied with beta-blockers, but they didn't completely steady the nerves. They could give you the strange impression of an underwater tsunami building beneath a calm surface.

The nerves were partly to do with uncertainty about the enterprise itself. I understood the concept of the workshop: people come together with shared tools and materials and an idea of making something lasting and serviceable – not a table or bed frame but the structure for a short story or a set of decorative metaphors. I loved that notion of building something together, and the comparison between writing and actual manufacture was pleasing. But did the analogy work? Writing is essentially a solitary task, one that only comes right after hours of trial and error. The tools and materials people need are already in their heads. The best examples to follow are on their shelves and in libraries. For Flannery O'Connor, 'the teacher's work should be largely negative ... We can learn how *not* to write.'

But it would be terrible to discourage novice writers

by pointing out their failings in public. 'The workshop leader's power can be huge, given that writing is so intimate,' writes A. L. Kennedy. 'Although the scale is tiny, the possibilities for wrongness and corruption can be appallingly extensive: ideas can be mocked, weaklings can be bullied, while tired or apprehensive participants can actively encourage the tutor to blather on about his or her self at revolting length and offer all the most toxic sorts of admiration.'

Best to start with something anodyne: 'Has everyone got a copy of the handout?' I shook the handout. Someone could always be relied upon not to have got the handout.

'Actually can I have one?' Sam asked, yawning and scratching his shoulder, leaving three claw marks above the Tamil tattoo.

'I'm interested to know what you all thought of the William Trevor extract.' I asked, then – in case nobody would think anything – followed up quickly with what I thought. 'Isn't it amazing how much information he manages to give about Leary in less than a hundred words?'

Nick began to count the words, moving his finger across the page.

'I liked the repetition of "spare" and "sparse", it's a sort of half-rhyme,' said Kisi, brightly. She had recently finished an English degree and knew the gist of these things.

'But why on earth doesn't he wear overalls?' Diana said sharply, as though discussing a staffing matter with the third secretary at the Embassy in Cairo.

'Could be significant,' said Tom, tapping his pen against his teeth. 'What does everyone else think?'

'He can't be bothered?' Jim suggested. 'Or he can't afford overalls?' Jim tended to treat our inquiries with an affable scepticism. He must have come on the course mainly to be with Jules.

'And what about the way Trevor lists all those different bits of Leary that have been stained from smoking,' I said. 'He could just have said "Leary's fingers were stained by nicotine".'

'So why didn't he?' asked Lynn. 'It would have been quicker.'

I said that I thought it was interesting to play with the reader's expectations, sometimes to give a lot of detail and sometimes to be unexpectedly vague. I mentioned *One Hundred Years of Solitude*, where rain falls in Macondo for four years, eleven months and two days, and *The Hitchhiker's Guide to the Galaxy*, where the meaning of life turns out to be '42'. The precision pulls you up short because it's not what you expect, I said. Giving things a numerical value seemed to assign them an importance we could see they didn't really have and that anomaly made us pay attention.

At the end of the table I saw Lily, the young insurance broker, scribbling these ideas down in her notepad and felt emboldened by my own authority.

'But then Leary is compared to an unspecified hedgerow animal. So Trevor's precise one moment and vague the next. Yesterday we talked about avoiding clichés and finding original ways to say things, but here Trevor dodges the problem altogether by not even trying to find an original comparison. You don't always have to nail the perfect description'

'It's probably a weasel,' said Nick.

'I was thinking of a hedgehog!' said Zoe brightly. She and Kisi had both painted their nails alternately blue and orange and I kept catching them flitting like butterflies at the edge of my vision.

'I don't think it would be a hedgehog,' said Nick, looking firmly at his notepad, a blush starting up around his ears. 'They're quite rare nowadays.'

'And weasels aren't?'

'Loads of weasels round Kent.'

'The point is that he lets you decide,' I said. 'What did you think about the way he uses a gadget to roll his cigarettes?'

'I've never actually even heard of that,' said Kisi.

'He doesn't trust himself to roll one freehand?' said Jim.

'Yes, or it could point to the fact that he is going to be manipulative,' I said. 'Later in the story.'

'I didn't get that,' said Sheena slowly shaking her head.

'You would only pick that up on a second reading, though, wouldn't you?' Diana said. 'Do you really think that a reader makes all those connections?'

'It's a good question. Perhaps not, but the image might stay in your subconscious. You could argue that some ideas inform our reading and writing without us even knowing it.' I was interested in the way secrets fuel writing and liked to feel that not everything in a book was obvious to the reader. The American poet Elizabeth Bishop advocated using one's experiences for inspiration in writing, while keeping the actual details private. Sometimes I wondered if it was dangerous to bring too much of your own life out into the light and not just because of the risk of harming others, though that was worrying too. You might end up a weaker writer, I thought, if you burned through that fuel. You might lose power, like Samson post-haircut.

'Of course it could also be that Trevor had no intention of suggesting anything like that,' I went on, 'He may simply have wanted to describe someone rolling a cigarette. Writers are allowed to use an image because they like it, and not because they want it to be analysed in a workshop.'

'It didn't do much for me. I thought it was boring,' said Lynn, arms tightly folded over ribs that were detectable under her thin sweater. A picture came to my mind then of Lynn at work in HR, handing people complex forms to fill in with a smirk of satisfaction. Perhaps she had rear-ranged the poem on the fridge. I felt an urge to say 'well you're wrong *Lynn*' or 'He is actually considered one of the greatest story-tellers of all time, *Lynn*.'

And then I was enveloped in a cherry-scented cloud of love. Jules was puffing on the beaded vape that hung around her neck, like a talisman discovered in a haul of precious antiquity. I smiled at Lynn. 'That's a totally valid response,' I said. 'Did you like the other extract?'

'Yeah kind of,' Lynn said grudgingly.

'The second passage is clearly set in wartime,' said Peter, scrutinizing his handout with a leer of concentration that forced more lines into an already crowded face, 'although the author – perhaps I should say authoress – doesn't tell us that it is.'

'It's a great example of the rule "show, don't tell",' said Tom. 'Sage doesn't tell us that her grandfather was a vicar, that she was a child during the Second World War, that her grandparents' relationship was violent. She lets us work those things out by showing us the vestments, the nasty scar.'

'Her grandparents really didn't like each other!' said Sheena, laughing and looking around her for corroboration.

'Can you please explain the "show, don't tell" rule?' said Diana, slapping the table with both palms, like someone who wants, without further ado, to put an end to some piece of nonsense. 'Why *can't* you tell? What's the difference?'

'I guess because it flattens the narrative?' said Tom. 'The reader likes to feel that they're working some things out for themselves.'

'Writing's a partnership,' I added. 'The author shouldn't do all the work or the reader loses interest.'

For that morning's exercise each person had to draw a floorpan of their childhood home, then swap it with the person sitting next to them who would mark a cross in one of the rooms. The assignment came in two parts: first to describe an object in that room. Then to use that description to lead into a piece of writing about a person or an event connected with that object.

'We'll take thirty minutes now, for the first part of the exercise and to get a coffee.'

I set off then towards the kitchen down a corridor lined with photographs of previous writers who had taught at the centre. Their treatment in black and white gave the subjects gravitas and glamour. These were the real writers, you couldn't help thinking. Later in the week Tom and I would be getting the black and white treatment too and I hoped for the same upgrading. I wondered what I should wear and wished I had brought a polo neck. Nora Ephron and Paul Auster always looked so good in theirs. Then fingers lightly touched my arm and I turned to find Susie approaching tentatively from behind.

'Can I have a word?'

'Of course. Let's go outside.'

We walked back to the main room and out into the garden, picking a bench at the side of the house. Susie was in her mid-fifties, pretty with bobbed grey hair and a slim figure that spoke of ballet lessons in youth, disciplined eating and a regular Pilates regime. Her face was pale and her grey eyes seemed to reflect some inner reluctance to make an impression. She was wearing a form-fitting linen dress and silver bangles that could just as easily have been bought in India as at a country fayre in the home counties. Susie was the kind of woman who, despite being beautiful, is often said to become invisible as she ages and seems to take invisibility as her lot.

'I think I'm going to leave,' Susie said, tilting her head in a kind of apology and, when she saw my face fall, she said quickly, 'It's nothing to do with you – it's my fault. I didn't realize that this was going to be so revealing.'

It was Wednesday, the day when people left. Occasionally they went without even saying goodbye. I hadn't expected Susie to be the one to go, though. I'd much rather Lynn took off.

'That would be such a shame Susie – please don't go. I haven't had a chance to read any of your writing yet. And it doesn't have to be revealing, you know.'

'The exercise you just set, about your childhood home . . .'

'That's just the home people tend to remember best. The exercise is about describing an object and a related incident. It doesn't have to be about anything significant or revealing. You could remember the tumble drier catching fire, or, I don't know, watching a television show. Not all memories are loaded.'

'OK. Yes, I suppose I see what you mean.'

'Most of the things that happen in homes are boring – but they can still lead to interesting observations.'

I thought of my mother's wrists, which were sometimes laced with thin burn marks from taking hot dishes out of the oven in fraying gloves. The marks seemed to stand both for the devotion and distraction of motherhood. Susie looked down at her own hands which lay submissively in her lap, as though waiting for the word: stay or leave.

'I'd feel sad if you left,' I said.

'Me too. I've had this planned for a long time. I've been thinking about writing for a while and my children have been nagging me to do something about it. They actually bought me this course as a birthday present.'

'Well then you have to stay. Plus you wanted to be pushed out of your comfort zone, right? You did say that on the first night.'

'I did,' Susie said, with a smile of recognition. 'But now I'm thinking my comfort zone was a nice place to be.'

'Look – I promise that you won't have to be more revealing than you want to be. And we're meeting together, this afternoon, aren't we?'

She nodded.

'So we can talk about your writing then. Let's go and get a coffee.'

Fear of exposure was a given in this kind of setting – you're being asked to read your work aloud; what could be more exposing? But in my experience many participants did in fact want to reveal themselves, even the ones who claimed otherwise. An idea had taken root in the general consciousness that 'creative writing' meant reaching into the soul to bring out secrets. Some tutors fed that need by encouraging their groups to explore terrible things that had happened to them, instead of writing about the more mundane aspects of life – the difficulty of walking a powerful dog, of administering a bed bath, of climbing up a broken escalator with no loss of dignity.

The things people do are as useful a route into character

as the way they feel. The glove factory in Philip Roth's *American Pastoral*, or the basketball game that opens John Updike's *Run, Rabbit*, contribute as much to the development of those novels' protagonists as any inner journey. But beginner writers often want to bypass the factory floor, the ball game and jump straight to the soul, without seeing that souls don't float free; they're anchored in bodies doing everyday things. And soulful investigations can make for dull writing; emotions are not only hard to describe but boring to read about when isolated from the other experiences of life because, in fact, they never are isolated from those things. Rachel Cusk's description of a tooth extraction in *Aftermath* is also about extracting herself from a marriage.

> The nurse hands him a chisel. He positions it on the edge of the jaw and places the flat tip between the tooth and the gum. He pushes down, straining so hard that his smile becomes a grimace. Presently he stands to improve his leverage. He uses both hands; he stands on tiptoe, bearing down with shaking arms. The tooth resists and resists, and when at last it gives way it does so too easily, so that the chisel spends its force upwards, hitting the teeth above.

People came to the writing school with unbearably sad stories, about children who had died, about surviving rape and suicide attempts, about addictions or parents who never loved them. Often they hoped to turn their own story into something that could be published, perhaps without realizing that also meant turning it into a package, a product that had to please publishing executives and marketing departments, that had to run the gauntlet of critics, then be sold in significant numbers to be a success. Publication might make things better or worse for them, but the strongest likelihood – as with any book – was that their story wouldn't get published at all. And the effect of that rejection might make them feel worse. Was it right, then, to encourage them down that road?

Perhaps there was an element of envy in what I hoped was mostly a protective instinct towards my students. I was drawn to write about the circumstances of my own life but had always felt it wouldn't be possible to do that without betraying or upsetting my family. I feared the instincts of a writer might overpower the instincts of a daughter, a sister. The idea that we can write about the events that shape us and not hurt other people in the process was appealing – I couldn't see a way to do it, though.

One creative writing teacher I knew briskly refused to let her sessions become therapeutic – 'That's very sad, but we're here to talk about writing' – and another had stopped teaching Life Writing because she found she didn't care about the stories any more, however sad. The deluge of grief and regret and missed chances had left her jaded.

It isn't always easy to tell apart the people who really do want to write a book from the ones who need a kindly ear.

But my feeling was that if someone wanted to write about sad events in their life, then talking about them was both a good preparation and a way to find out whether those experiences would – or should – make a publishable book. Writing about your feelings doesn't require the imprimatur of publication.

My one-to-one sessions took place in the shed, a window-less stone outhouse that had once been a byre or a stable. There was just room for a desk and two chairs. Sun poured in at the doorway through which the resident ruminant would once have looked out at hills and fields. The door-way itself was so small that everyone who appeared in it darkened it, blotting out the sun as they stepped forward, holding notepads and printed pages. A lot of them also brought a cup of tea.

By mid-afternoon I was awash, but you can't turn down a cup of goodwill. I had been talking to Zoe and Kisi about the book on festivals they wanted to write and was in a cheerful mood, infected by their enthusiasm. Their idea had potential – they had already planned a summer visit-ing festivals large and small around the country, charting their experiences while also exploring the social history of festivals, their evolution from ad-hoc rural gatherings to corporate events dominated by wealthy white people. They wanted to explore that paradox, common to so many events – creative writing courses too – by which something that begins as a chaotic, collective endeavour is tidied up and turned into a commercial product. Zoe and Kisi were beautiful, marketable, and their book could be filled with photographs of more beautiful people enjoying themselves in a modern medieval setting. Round the table in the shed we had started working up the first draft of a summary that could be used as a pitch for agents, plus ideas for two short pieces that could make newspaper or magazine features. Kisi was going to write about the battles during her teenage years with her Ghanaian parents to be allowed to go to any kind of music event; Zoe was planning a piece on drug culture.

They went off to work on their ideas in a sunny spot in the garden, then Susie walked in very upright, like someone trying not to spill a liquid. At first I thought it was the tea she was trying not to spill. But as soon as she sat down tears dropped over the rims of her pale eyes.

'I'm sorry about earlier,' she said, hurriedly brushing them away. 'It's all been quite a lot to deal with.'

'This week, or . . . ?'

'Well, the last few years, really!' she said, with a laugh that turned into a kind of hiccup and made her apologize again. She told me that her husband had left her five years ago, not long after their twenty-fifth wedding anniversary. Susie had been bewildered by his decision to go; they had a happy marriage, she said, and still had sex – she lowered her voice for this revelation. To make things worse, he had left with one of her best friends, a woman who ran a livery stable in the next village. Her husband's defence, that he wanted a last chance at happiness, casually wrote their marriage off as unhappy, when Susie felt sure that wasn't how he had experienced it. Her hunch that this was some kind of mid-life crisis seemed borne out by the fact that, a year after leaving, her husband had got back in touch, saying that he thought he had made a mistake, that he wanted to see her again. But then he had died suddenly, after a heart attack, and it fell to his new partner to arrange the funeral without involving her. Susie and her children had sat at the back of the church, like any other guest.

'I suppose I should at least be grateful that we got to go,' Susie said.

'That's incredibly sad, though. I'm so sorry.' I reached to touch Susie's arm and the silver bangles shivered. It was important to give the moment its due and not start thinking how this story could be turned into writing although that, in the end, was what we were here for, and there were only twenty minutes before the next person appeared in the doorway. Susie's story – a love of many years, thrown away on a whim then cut off just as it might have been reprised – had potential. It was a tragedy for both of them, because the husband's last-ditch dash for adventure was as understandable, however foolish and cruel, as the wife's devastation. Fear, vanity and selfishness make people do terrible things to each other. For thousands of years these have been the engines of stories. But there was no discernible arc to this particular one; Susie would have to be a good writer to make it fill two hundred pages.

'Is this something you would really like to write about?' I asked.

'It depends on what you mean by ...' She sniffed and briskly straightened up. 'I suppose I want to make sense of it.'

'Even if it's painful revisiting that time?'

'Yes,' she nodded. 'I think so.'

'Have you started writing it? Have you got it with you?'

'No. There's not really anything to show. I keep starting it, then abandoning it. I can't make it work. I don't even know how to go about it, to be honest.'

'What about if you put it aside and start somewhere else – take the pressure off. You could write regularly in a notebook – or keep a diary – do you ever do that?'

'Not really,' Susie shook her head. 'Not for ages.'

'It might help you identify what you're good at and what you're interested in. You could try writing every day, about the things that happen, the things you think about. Use the diary to explore your feelings and memories and see what ideas come out of that. If you write regularly, some theme may emerge that takes you in the direction of a longer piece. Then maybe you could aim for a feature, or an essay.'

'I was also wondering about writing a novel,' Susie said, as though she had just decided that in fact fiction was the answer, and she wiped the tears over her cheeks, making them glisten. On both sides her bob came to neat points beneath her chin, a sympathetic frame for the despond-ent face.

'OK, but that's a completely different approach,' I said, shifting position. My back was beginning to ache from the hard wood chair on the hard stone floor. 'You mean fictionalizing your experience? Or writing something different inspired by it? Or just totally different?'

'What do you think?'

'I think making stuff up is harder.'

It was like being a doctor sometimes, sitting there at my desk, hearing about symptoms and trying to locate their source, dispensing advice while discreetly keeping an eye on the clock. In some cases the diagnosis people wanted was simple: 'Have I got it, doctor? Have I got a story?'

Perhaps it was a symptom of our age. More and more people wanted to tell their story. Every few years a new survey would come out, suggesting that at least three quarters of Americans or Britons wanted to write a book, quite brazenly, you might think considering how few of them, according to other surveys, regularly read books. A significant chunk of the population apparently believed, with a chutzpah verging on arrogance, that they could write a book despite never reading any. Why? From my own experience, people who signed up for writing courses had often been assured by friends that they had a story to tell. Sheena, for example, had said she wouldn't be here if not for work colleagues urging her to 'tell your story'.

Then again, everyone who thinks they have a story is right: they do. The woman with an eating disorder who wants to rescue donkeys has a story. The man whose character changed after a riding accident has a story. So does the woman who sued her builders after a botched loft extension, or the man who met his future partner in a bowling alley, or the couple who accidentally threw away their winning lottery ticket. These are the stories we hear every day. Some people are really good at telling them, polishing them up for entertainment value. Even when they embark on an anecdote to which we all know the end, we still want to hear them tell it. Others have harnessed technology, unrolling their stories in posts or tweets that gather likes as they progress. Mobile phones have been a gift both to storytellers and their audiences. To witness the top deck of a bus fall silent as one woman spits into a phone, 'I know what you did and I'll never trust you again', and then unwinds a tale of eye-watering duplicity and infidelity, is to experience story-telling of the highest order. I've even diverted from my route to work to hear the end of a promising story, like the one told by a man swaggering across the concourse at Waterloo Station, whose anecdote ended: 'It took five men to hold him down and they found the package up his arse.'

Everyone has a story inside, but in most cases extraction proves too difficult, even for talented writers; because having a story isn't the same as being able to fill a hundred, two hundred or three hundred pages with incident and atmosphere, to create breathing characters, to calibrate the tension, hit the moments of revelation at the right time and shape a narrative arc that sometimes seems as elusive as a double rainbow. Learning how to change one word for another, to think about the rhythm and heft of a sentence – these are all part of the package.

Once I taught an alcoholic, a great writer on the love of booze, the hatred of it, the terrible things it had made him do to other people, his cold fear on waking up in a police station with no recollection of what had happened the night before. He never succeeded in gathering those stories together for publication, but I really wish he had.

Sam came after Susie, full of tales about his wonderful year of travel, tales that were unlikely to add up to a book, although we talked about ideas for features.

Then Jules arrived, bearing tea and biscuits. She was easy to please because she had no ambitions to publish, only to enjoy writing. She showed me a piece written in a hurry, she said, because she and Jim had spent the afternoon reading Agatha Christie to each other in bed. My mind was busy with this image for most of the time I was meant to be helping her. Though much the same age as Susie, she exuded fulfilment and new love.

My last session of the day was with Nick. The evening sun glinted kindly on his glasses as he stood at the door to the shed, holding a thick wad of papers.

'Is this a whole novel?' I asked, as the manuscript thudded down in front of me.

Nick nodded modestly.

'Impressive. Not many people manage to get to the end. Congratulations!'

'It's the novel I wrote about the last course I was on.'

'Really? About the actual course? The course itself?'

Sitting in the shed, which was several degrees colder than the garden outside, I began to look through the manuscript, first noticing a word, an expletive towards the more violent end of things, the odd incursion on the page then more and more of them – cunt, tits, cum, cock. I read some of the paragraphs. There were sex acts on every page, apparently not linked by any kind of narrative or thread, except that the three participants so imaginatively involved in penetrating one another were the two tutors who had taught the last class Nick had been on, plus their invited guest that week. The byre grew chilly. More offensive than the sex was the absence of any kind of story. Nick's book wasn't a book at all. It was gibberish. A four hundred-page fantasy.

The imperative to look up from the page and meet Nick's eye felt impossibly weighty. I made myself do it.

'I actually know one of these writers,' I said, because I couldn't think of anything else to say.

'Yes, I remember you told me on the first night.' Nick's face brightened politely. His hair was neatly cut and I was struck by the thought that someone would get a good haircut then go home to write riotous filth about rogering the creative writing tutor. My instinct was to feel sorry for him, but what if he was one of those pathetic types who threatened women online, telling them they were going to be raped, or they should be raped, or they were, on reflection, too ugly to rape? There was a wider margin between Nick's ears and his hairline than looked quite right. Perhaps this was a message from the barber to warn people off. There was also a stippling of rough red skin, razor burn maybe, around his jawline.

'I think you should change her name. All the names. You know, in case these people didn't want to be in your novel.'

'OK. Yes, I can easily do that.' Nick produced a notebook from his shirt pocket and carefully wrote this advice down. The presence of the notebook brought a pressure to make more helpful comments, but it seemed wrong to give serious attention to a book that couldn't be a book, this would-be – but definitely wouldn't-be – novel.

'So what's the next one about?'

'I'm going to write about this course, too.'

'Really? So you're writing about courses as you take them. That's an interesting, um, approach, to the whole writing-course idea.'

I meant it as a joke, but Nick nodded gravely. Perhaps he had never got the point of writing courses: he thought they existed to provide, not guidance, but actual material for books. It was embarrassing to think he might involve Tom and me in the kind of lewd acts he had subjected those other writers to. He had better change our names, at least.

'I mean I can see the attraction. You have a ready-made cast of characters, the country house setting is a classic . . .'

'There's going to be a double murder in this one,' Nick said.

73

'Whoa! Intriguing! Well I'll look forward to that!'

When our twenty minutes were over, I hurried back to the house and up to the part of it where Tom and I had our rooms. He had finished his sessions for the day and was already sitting with a glass of wine at his desk. He and I had each been given a bottle of wine when we arrived and were guarding them in our rooms although there were more bottles downstairs, each labelled for the course participant who had paid for it. Tom's room was a mirror image of mine: large wardrobe, double bed, a desk by the window and some black-and-white portraits of self-confident looking previous tutors. Jackie Kay smiling but strong. Will Self, an angry tangle of limbs and crumpled intensity. They would both have known how to handle Nick.

'Hey, how was your afternoon?'

'Nick might be unhinged,' I gasped, sitting down on the bed.

'Only Nick? Surely a few of them—'

I told him about the four hundred obscene pages, about Nick's plan to write about our course, about the double murder. Tom swung his legs off the desk and sat forward, frowning.

'I'm not saying people shouldn't write porn,' I said, 'but this was insanely—'

'God.'

'*Violent* . . .'

'Shit.'

'Just, *formless*. Porn needs some minimum storyline,

right? Not that I'm an expert. Anyway, I don't feel this is the place, am I being—'

'No, it's obviously not,' said Tom. 'Should we say something?'

'I don't know. I don't know if he's done anything wrong. I mean—'

'It's definitely inappropriate.'

Inappropriate. The dread word that hung over so many activities nowadays. I would rather resign myself than eject Nick for being inappropriate.

'He seems fine in the workshops. Just quiet,' Tom said.

'He did say there are a lot of weasels in Kent.'

'Not certifiable in itself.'

'I'd hate to call him out when he hasn't really done anything. Then again, he said he's going to write about this course, too, and that someone will be murdered.'

'Christ. Look, I'm sure there's nothing to worry about. Have some wine.'

'It's OK, I'll get mine in a minute. Then I might go and count the knives in the kitchen drawer.'

'Hey, come on.'

'It's a joke! Did you see Diana today, by the way?'

'Yes. Why?'

'No reason, I was wondering what her aunty's letters were like.'

'Right.'

'I've got a dread of things found in attics – diaries, letters . . .'

'Why? There's all kinds of good stuff to be found in attics, no?'

'Of course – but are two thousand people going to shell out twenty quid for your aunty's letters? They'd have to be so incredibly revealing in some way. I don't want her to be disappointed if they aren't publishable.'

'She didn't bring the letters, actually, just a monograph on an Egyptian artist she's interested in.'

'Perhaps she's saving them for me.'

'And Peter spent half his session pointing out things I got wrong in my book.'

'He did the same to me! He must have been combing them for mistakes.'

'He's a good writer though. Look, if you're worried about Nick, you could call your friend, the one who taught him, and see what she says.'

'Good idea.'

It turned out that my friend remembered Nick clearly. 'He's barking,' she said, 'but harmless.'

We decided not to go to the centre director about Nick, but then he came to see us before leaving for the night – he and the other staff lived off-site – to tell us that that evening's entertainment had been cancelled. A writer had been supposed to visit, to read aloud from his work and answer questions, but his train had broken down and he had been forced to turn back. The guest appearance was usually a highlight of the week, although I sometimes felt that the group was less welcoming than they might be. Historian Lucy Hughes-Hallett had been left sitting in a room on her own. The explorer Benedict Allen had been asked to change a lightbulb 'since you're so tall'. Much later Allen had stripped off his clothes to reveal the tribal markings he acquired when travelling in Papua New Guinea – another late-night revelation I had missed.

'Oh, and another thing, bit annoying, this,' the centre director said. 'Lynn's decided to leave. She's put in a complaint.'

'She's done what?' said Tom, pretending to slam down his wine glass.

'What's the complaint about?' I asked, defensively.

The centre director leaned into the door jamb. 'It's nothing you need to worry about. She just said she's finding it boring. She said she's on holiday and had thought there would be more fun activities.'

'Fun activities? Does she want a water slide?'

'Like I said, nothing to worry about. She can put it on the feedback form and—'

'It's not as if it's a holiday for everyone,' Tom interrupted, 'Some people here seriously want to be published.'

'Exactly,' I said, 'we're trying to give everyone something useful.'

The centre director made mollifying gestures. He tended to wear mollifying jumpers. Jumpers designed to reassure, to defuse tensions, to make the unlovable feel loved; jumpers with a whiff of Ted Hughes.

'Of course,' he said and, spreading his hands, 'Look, there's always someone.'

'Anyone else complain?' I said.

'Not really. Peter thinks the wine should be included in the cost of the course. Zoe wants to borrow a charger. It's that level of stuff.'

We needed another entertainment for the evening. At dinner Diana suggested a game of literary charades, which sounded risky, but she took charge, splitting us into two groups and shooing her own team out of the room with the brisk movements of an experienced stockwoman. I hoped that we were about to gain some insight into after-dinner life at the British Embassy in Cairo.

Minutes later her team burst into the room prowling and snarling.

'I know – *Company of Wolves*!' said Kisi, bouncing on the sofa in a way that reminded you she had quite recently been a child.

'*Going on a Bear Hunt*!' shouted Jules, from her armchair, blonde spillage of curls around her shoulders.

Then the people who had been prowling and snarling withdrew to the sides of the room and Nick came to stand in front of us. His only job was to stand and point towards the door.

'*The Idiot*!' trumpeted Peter.

I hardly dared look at Nick, but he seemed to giggle at this response, shoulders heaving as he tried to keep pointing with a steady hand. I was worrying now that, in scorning Nick's incoherent pornography, I had failed to recognize a work of modernist genius. What if he were the next Michel Houellebecq? I had to make sure Tom read his manuscript too, in case he thought differently. The book made no sense, though, unless it made a kind of sense that I hadn't been clever enough to see. Perhaps I was too bourgeois to get it, I thought miserably, remembering that Houellebecq despised the bourgeoisie. At the very least he should have changed the names, though. And then I remembered, with rising indignation, some of the more lurid scenarios in Nick's manuscript and decided he really didn't deserve my sympathy. He would have me bound, trussed, raped and murdered in his next novel. And not even change my name.

'*Wolf Hall*!' shouted Peter, baring his own canines.

It was the right answer and everyone fell smiling out of character.

Exercise Two

Keeping a Diary

January

'Arrange whatever pieces come your way' wrote Virginia Woolf in her diary, and it's good advice, even when the pieces – a half-remembered conversation, the subtext of a smile – seem at first not to lead anywhere. They can go in a notebook or diary until the meaning becomes clear, perhaps not until months or years later. I've got a drawer full of notebooks, yet I rarely have one with me when I need it. When I'm in the thick of a project ideas come all the time, but they're more likely to strike in the middle of the supermarket, or on a walk, than at my desk. So now I'll stop, wherever I am – under a tree, beside Frozen Goods, at a bus shelter – and note the thought down on any scrap of paper I can find in my bag – a receipt, the back of a ticket, the inside of a paracetamol box. I don't bother putting my glasses on, just scrawl it down.

It might be a few days before I come to decipher the words, excited by the memory of the creative thunderbolt that interrupted my shopping or walking. But often the meaning has vanished in the same puff of smoke with which it appeared. 'Like a caterpillar', says my note, or 'because he can't and he never could'. Or months, later, I'll open the paracetamol packet and find 'hairy shins' written inside, like a taunt. When there's no paper or pen handy, I send myself cryptic texts and emails that land in my inbox like anonymous tipoffs – 'she couldn't have done it because she didn't know until later.' The emails are easier to read than the scrawled notes, and they have a kind of authority, as though they were written by someone who really knew what she was talking about although, unfortunately, she hadn't had time to explain it.

Lots of writers find walking a useful way to make sense of the pieces. Woolf would walk halfway across London on an invented pretext ('I must buy a pencil'). She called this activity 'street haunting'. Charles Dickens might walk twenty miles in a day, or all through the night. In *Night Walks* he describes passing the Bethlehem mental asylum in Beckenham and wondering if darkness brought the people inside it and outside closer. 'Are not the sane and the insane equal at night as the sane lie a dreaming?'

My brother may have walked for several hours through

East London before jumping to his death from a building in Deptford. My sister, who herself became mentally ill some years later, dealt with her disquiet by walking. Once, she told us, she walked along Kensington High Street and saw the ghosts of people who had walked there in the past. We brought her home then. We needed to look after her.

Around this time I was referred to a genetic counsellor. The woman was kind and reassuring, she saw no reason to worry about having children. I was the one who was more likely to be affected by mental ill health, she said. Where two siblings have a major mental illness, the third has a strong chance of being similarly affected. Had my brother ever received a diagnosis? I said that he hadn't, but I didn't really know. I was afraid to ask.

Perhaps all of us walk among ghosts, along haunted streets. Oxford Street and Piccadilly teem with unseen millions. We brush past Virginia Woolf in Russell Square and Charles Dickens on the Strand. We glimpse shadowy figures at the end of ancient alleyways. We're connected with the past and future – but we can't always make sense of the connections.

Today I went to buy bras with some money just in from the *Times Literary Supplement*.

In a cubicle near Oxford Street a small, smartly dressed woman stared thoughtfully at my naked reflection.

'Tell me about your boobs,' she said.

'Sorry, my . . . ?'

'Books. What kind of books do you write?'

Marcella had been a bra fitter for twenty years, first in Milan and now in London and must have learned that conversation makes things easier. She would have asked an estate agent about property and a barrister about crime, so it made sense to talk to a writer about books. I told her about my books and translations. 'My non-fiction books are what they call "travel literature",' I said. I would have used air quotes, but that was awkward while bending over with Marcella adjusting the straps from behind. I might have looked like someone trying to fly, or reenact that scene from *Titanic*. 'Then there are two novels.'

As I stood up, our eyes met in the mirror. 'I don't think this balconette is for you,' Marcella said. She was wearing a plain black shift, and had the old-fashioned look of a couturier's seamstress. You could imagine her holding pins between her lips. In line with her understated appearance, her face was deliberately free of make-up and was beautiful. Her reflection must have seemed a graceful riposte to some of the high-gloss faces that blew in off Oxford Street.

'So tell me what is your style?'

'For bras?'

'No, books.'

'OK. I suppose, well, literary fiction.'

'Lit-er-all-y friction. Literary friction,' Marcella repeated. 'I think this full cup will be a better look. What does it mean, literary friction?'

What does it mean? What *does* it mean? I wasn't all that

sure myself. I looked away. How embarrassing to have to talk about my books with no top on.

'There's a lot of description,' I said apologetically. 'The way the story is told is more important than the story itself.'

'I think you are a Prima Donna,' said Marcella, sweeping out of the cubicle.

She came back with another lacey armful and there was a whole hour of this – bending and scooping, submitting to Marcella's scrutiny before I left holding a tiny bag. Outside the Christmas lights were still up on Oxford Street and shops in central London had been twinkling with decorations for three months. Christmas, which has been maximized for the twenty-first century, starts in mid October now, to please the tourists, and ends in the middle of January. I walked up Oxford Street through crowds of people glumly negotiating the sales. 'The garishness and gaudiness of the great rolling ribbon of Oxford Street has its fascination,' wrote Virginia Woolf in 1931. 'A thousand such voices are always crying aloud in Oxford Street. All are tense, all are real, all are urged out of their speakers by the pressure of making a living, finding a bed, somehow keeping afloat on the bounding, careless, remorseless tide of the street.'

I had an appointment to speak to some Creative Writing students at the University of Westminster. It's one of the ironies of the writing life that a subsection of people who don't like speaking find themselves needing to do it for money. 'We've advertised it right across the faculty,' said

84

the English Department lecturer who met me in the foyer. 'It's going to be in the Grand Hall.'

The Grand Hall. I would have preferred the Small Hall. In the Ladies I remembered the friend who had vomited while miked up, just before giving a talk. I wondered how many writers carry hip flasks or tranquillizers and why I wasn't one of them. I looked in the mirror and thought very hard of Angela Merkel. Christine Lagarde and Michelle Obama are also good role models for the anxious public speaker, but Merkel's my favourite because she never looks comfortable under the public gaze and yet she manages to keep going, while Lagarde and Obama seem unreachably poised.

The last time I spoke to an audience of people under twenty it was to a class of ten-year-olds at my children's primary school. 'What questions would you like to ask Miss?' the teacher said and a boy asked: 'Are you rich enough to own a stretch limo?'

'No!' I said, and laughed, before turning to another child to receive a more serious question, but then this one asked, 'How many more books do you think you will have to write before you can afford to buy a stretch limo?' Then somebody in the row behind said that she had been in a stretch limo on her sister's birthday but it was just rented and that she'd heard you would need at least a billion pounds to buy one; then a boy at the back of the class said nonchalantly that his father was a quantity surveyor and could easily afford a stretch limo if he wanted one.

That was when I lost the room and the conversation went from one about books to one about limousines and how much money you would need to buy one and whether or not J. K. Rowling owned one and how you would accessorize your limousine once you had it. The teacher watched on indulgently, feeling no obligation to steer the conversation back to books. I wasn't even getting paid. No bra money in this gig.

A girl at the front said she would have a glitter-ball and a fridge in her limousine. A boy said that he would get the biggest TV screen possible and ride around town watching films with his friends and eating popcorn.

'What colour one would you have, Miss, if you could afford one?' someone asked.

'Black, I suppose, but I don't—'

'That's boring Miss! You should have a pink one.'

And then I said haughtily that I didn't want a limousine and that, even if I could make enough money from writing to buy one, I wouldn't get one. And that was the moment – sometimes these moments can be pinpointed – when I fatally lost all authority. The children couldn't respect a person who disdained limousines.

This audience of eighteen- and nineteen-year-old Creative Writing students was much kinder. They sat respectfully through my reading and only one fell asleep. At 11 a.m., it was both too late and too early to be tired, but at least she was diplomatic, drifting off with her forehead pressed against one splayed hand, brow slightly furrowed, so that it looked as though she wasn't sleeping but immersed in concentration.

A young woman in a headscarf asked, 'Does everyone have a story to tell?'

'Yes, I think so,' I said. 'The difficult part is telling it.'

February

Two days a week I teach writing skills to the clinical staff of a large hospital. Teaching scientists is a different challenge from teaching creative writers. Here's an area of life where it's crucially important to be clear. While a novelist may ponder colourful ways to describe a sunset, a bunion, a sense of despair, there is only one way to describe extracorporeal membrane oxygenation, and you'd better get it right. The stakes are higher, too. Bad writing in science could lead to the wrong treatment. In fiction it might only kill your career.

There are some similarities between teaching would-be novelists and scientists. In both cases the writer needs to be reminded that they have a reader, that the writing represents a relationship and not just a monologue. But there are important differences, too. Scientists have to be warned against getting into linguistic tangles, while tangles can be good for novelists. Scientists must aim for the truth. They shouldn't think of ten different ways to explain a phenomenon but only one, clear and truthful way. Novelists should always be looking for new ways to tell the truth.

Any minute now I expect to join the hospital NFAs – the staff who have 'no fixed abode'. There aren't enough places for everyone to work and I'm forever defending my space, constantly at risk of losing my desk.

For the moment I can't complain. I share a big office with windows onto the street. On the walls are motivational quotes from Steve Jobs, the Dalai Lama and God.

'It doesn't make sense to hire smart people and then tell them what to do; we hire smart people so they can tell us what to do.' (Steve Jobs)

'Be kind whenever possible, it is always possible.' (Dalai Lama)

'For I know the plans I have for you. They are plans for good and not for disaster, to give you a future and a hope.' (God)

My colleague, who put the posters up, might say that they are there to encourage people who come in and happen to see them, but I suspect they were chosen to send a message specifically to her manager, who visits daily and has to sit facing them. The insinuation is that she is overworked and undervalued. Another poster, which I find myself studying when my colleague is out of the room, has the title 'The Success Indicator' and shows the outlines of two people embodying the qualities of a successful and an unsuccessful person. The successful person, who is a woman, stands tall and looks foxy in a suit. She is successful, among other reasons, because she 'exudes joy', 'reads every day' and 'keeps a journal'. The unsuccessful person – a man, incidentally – is crouched low to convey his mendacity and self-loathing. This unsuccessful person, the poster says 'bears grudges', 'operates from a transactional perspective' and 'watches TV every day'. One of the worst things about unsuccessful people, though, is that 'they say they keep a journal but they really don't'.

That strikes me as a harsh measure of someone's personality. Who hasn't claimed sometimes to keep a diary, hoping that the intention may crystallize into action? I seem to fall between these two positions – standing and crouching – as I do read most days but I also watch TV. Some years I am better at keeping a diary than others. Exuding joy every day is a big ask.

My days in this office are numbered anyway. Last week a woman came in with a tape measure and started making calculations around me as I sat there typing, and it was like being measured up for a coffin. 'We could get four more people in here,' she called to her colleague, over my head. Soon we will be expected to relinquish designated spaces and sit wherever we can find a chair and a monitor. This mad scramble for a seat used to be called 'hot desking'. Now it's been rebranded as 'agile working' and is supposed to be seen as fun – an opportunity to mix things up. Z, who is small and bald and sits in the next door office, is an ally. 'Keep smilling beutiful' he sometimes emails me. He makes me tea even when I have said that I don't want any, and once he left an apple on my desk, making me feel like a 1950s school teacher.

March

I'm writing at home today, staring out of the window at the woman who works at her desk in the window opposite, imagining an endless, repeating pattern of women at desks, like an Escher print or a Borges story. Perhaps we are all writing the same book; we may all be stuck on the same sentence.

Over the last twenty years our area has evolved from a scruffy corner of South London to a French enclave where every other shop sells either cashmere or baby clothes, and some even sell cashmere clothes for babies. Once there were two fishmongers, three butchers, four or five greengrocers and corner shops stocking every kind of spice and any conceivable gizmo you might need for the home. Shops not much bigger than an average living room stocked an array of contraptions for catching rats. There was an ironmonger who stood in front of dozens of drawers for different kinds of nail or screw. There were Caribbean grocers with big boxes of yam and plantain on the pavement. One of the fishmongers provided a chair for elderly customers to sit in and pass the time of day.

The fruit and vegetable shops sold out to Starbucks, Space NK and All Bar One. The ironmonger became a noodle place, then a pasta place, a pizza place, a burger place and now a Thai place. The Post Office turned into a succession of high street clothes shops no one ever visited and is presently unoccupied while locals rage about the difficulty of posting anything. The Fried Chicken joint, which everyone imagined to be a front for drug-dealing, since they never made any chicken there, sells beauty products now. The chair has gone and the Caribbean community is moving out. Our irascible butcher is still a fixture, in his long blood-smattered smock, growling at customers who get on his bad side. He loathes people who ask for lamb shanks, regarding this as a trendy fad and a wasteful way to cut meat.

There used to be a charity shop at the bottom of our street from which it was generally acknowledged that no money ever found its way to charity. Every evening the elderly shopkeeper wheeled a barrow of the best donations, huffing and puffing, up our street and back to her house, a hoarder's paradise. She never turned down anything, and so was very popular with declutterers. We still have plenty of charity shops and doubtless they are more honest, but they're picky as hell. For example they hate books. I try to sneak them through under a pile of clothes, although apparently if you give them to Oxfam they can be sold for road surfacing.

My friend A said she was walking down a road in Brixton yesterday when a man said, 'Hello sexy, do you want me to show you a good time?'

'No thank you!' she said – startled, but not forgetting her manners – and hurried on towards her house. But afterwards she wondered if she should have asked what kind of good time was on offer. 'It's not like you often get the chance nowadays.' We debated whether the man may have thought she was a prostitute, or may himself have been drunk or mentally ill, pursuing these explanations for some time before it occurred to me that it was rude to suggest my friend could only appear attractive to a stranger in one of these circumstances.

'You know what? We haven't considered the possibility that he genuinely thought you were sexy, and sincerely wanted to show you a good time?'

My friend laughed so hard she almost choked on her coffee. As far as she was concerned that was not even a faint possibility, and B, who I saw later on, seemed to agree. 'We can't be fanciable at our age,' she pronounced. And yet she told me the other day that she spends fortunes on grooming. And sometimes she talks about surgery, too. 'You know I never would, but it's tempting.'

Wherever middle-aged women gather together, this conversation is likely to come up. We wonder what we would do, where we would draw the line, because we don't know what kind of old ladies we're going to be. The past may be a foreign country, but at least it's one we've all been to and from which we may conserve some treasured mementoes – the psychic equivalents of a bottle of Ouzo, a fridge magnet, a snow dome. Old age is a blank page. It's hard to think yourself into that state, even as we all move steadily towards it, like a herd of goats advancing together across the Gobi desert towards the Zambezi. What will we do? Will we go for fillers and sprinkles? Will we wear our glasses on a chain, slide gratefully into elasticated waistbands?

April

This morning I had to give a PowerPoint presentation on writing skills to a hall full of healthcare scientists. My host handed me a microphone 'so you can walk around and not get stuck behind the desk'. No sooner had he said this than I knew that I was doomed to get stuck behind the desk. For the first ten slides I was simultaneously talking about grammar and sentence structure while waging an internal battle, willing my legs to walk away from the desk, finding them incapable of doing so.

They say that people fear public speaking almost as much as death. For me both signify a moment of existential crisis. Even a simple presentation in front of a friendly audience is enough to trigger a thought process in which I end up examining whole areas of my life – character flaws, mistakes made years ago, failures both professional and personal. It's like a story by Clarice Lispector in which an apparently stable world collapses without warning into a horrifying chasm of despair.

In the hour before I'm due to arrive at the venue I may find myself sitting on a bench somewhere nearby, drinking energy drinks and eating energy bars, gearing myself up for the ordeal as though it were an Arctic trek. I know that at 6 p.m. I'm going to get up and walk to the lecture theatre for a sound check, but in another scenario that seems almost as plausible, I stay sitting on the bench. Six o'clock comes and goes and then six-thirty. I stay on the bench all evening, until night falls and I slump sideways, pull my coat around me and sleep fitfully. Next morning I may still be on the bench and stay there for successive days, until the world around me stops making any sense: the people hurrying through Russell Square shooting glances my way, the foreign students in their protective groups. A pair of police officers may approach and ask me what my name is, where I live, and I may not be able to tell them. They'll notice the incongruity of my smart clothes and the urine pooled under the bench, look through my bag and find my PowerPoint presentation and the notes about writing skills and contact the organization where I was due to speak.

It's only the dread of this experience, the contest of horrifying scenarios in which public speaking comes off as marginally less awful, that prompts me to get up at 5.55 p.m. and walk to the lecture hall. Of course, once I get going, I'm usually fine, but the same may also be true of death.

My office colleague has been stepping up her hostility. Today I arrived at the office and there was no keyboard attached to the computer. I sat and looked pointlessly at the screen for a while, too scared to ask for help from my room mate, who was typing furiously on her own keyboard. 'I bet she took it,' I thought to myself. 'The Dalai Lama wouldn't call that kind.' Eventually I went next door and asked Z to help me. He immediately produced a keyboard and set everything up and afterwards wrote to say that he would help me whenever I wanted. 'It's never a problem.' I wanted to cry with gratitude.

Today I arrived at work to find a woman at my desk who said it has been permanently assigned to her. She was wearing a tag that said Head of Leadership, making her somehow incontestable. 'I'm so sorry,' she said, 'I've never known exactly who you are.'

Even leaders have to understand grammar, I thought bitterly, as I sloped off to have a coffee with someone I know in HR. She told me of a little room she thinks I can use while I continue my residency. We took a lift up to the eighth floor and found it at the top of the building, a sterile room with no motivational quotes on the wall and very quiet, probably because nobody knows where it is. If I ever get locked in no one will hear the cries for help. I may be discovered decades from now, a grammar handout clutched in my wizened hand.

An email from Z arrived: Keep Smilling.

May

It's hot and the squares of central London are suddenly filled with women in bikinis. Long white hairy legs protrude from Speedos. Naked children splash in fountains. In Gordon Square the ghost of Virginia Woolf could be seen fanning herself on a bench. Hot days seem to come unexpectedly in this time of climate change, say after a week of hail and just before a spell of snow. Everyone gets caught on the hop. People who had been going about in thermal underwear and winter clothes race to lie naked in the nearest park knowing, from experience, that they have about forty hours before the weather turns. Then, a few days later it starts snowing and people say cheerfully, 'Well, that was our summer, then.' That rueful observation is almost as much a part of being British in the summer as strawberries and deckchairs.

The writing life can be lonely so I feel a kinship with the woman who sits at her desk across the way from my window, even though she is much more glamorous. She wears her hair in an elegant chignon and conducts video conversations in which she gesticulates in a charming way. I always suspected she was French and now that spring is here and the windows are opened, her voice confirms the fact.

The French are the second largest community in this neighbourhood now, and the Jehovah's Witnesses hand out as many copies of *Reveille!* as they do *Awake!* The other day a smart family of four came to the front door and the man asked me:

'*Vous parlez français?*'

'*Oui*,' I said, smugly. I hoped that they were in some kind of difficulty that I could help solve. Perhaps they were lost, or locked out, or urgently needed to buy a baby some cashmere.

Vous avez besoin de cachemire pour votre bébé? Suivez-moi!

But no, the question was even more urgent than that.

'*Croyez-vous qu'il y a une vie après la mort?*' said the man.

We must have covered that subject in an A-level French conversation class, but I wasn't sure how to reprise it now, on my doorstep, with no preparation.

'*Je parle français, mais je ne suis pas française,*' I explained. 'Also, some other people came round last week. I've already got the magazine.'

Today Z, who has been sending motivational emails every day – 'keep smilling!' 'enjoy you day!' – asked me out for a coffee and I agreed to go. I am isolated in my room on the eighth floor and people with appointments have difficulty finding me so I'm grateful to be remembered. But there was also an ulterior motive in meeting Z: I thought he might know how to get me, if not a better desk, then at least computer access, which I am currently without. I can't get onto the intranet and if you can't get on the intranet, you're nobody here. Z works on the IT for Compliance. He spends all day on the intranet.

I waited outside the cafe where we had agreed to meet and saw Z bounding across the square in his leather jacket, looking very much like someone who knows how to resolve

IT problems. But once we were sitting down with our coffees he seemed uninterested in my complaints about the desk and the computer, then out of the blue, he asked me if I would like to go for dinner and dancing at a restaurant near his home in Hertfordshire. I made a few incoherent sounds to the effect that that wasn't going to be possible. What about lunch, then, he said, as a Christmas present? I said no, I didn't think so and the conversation became strained.

Later, back on the eighth floor, an email arrived from Z saying that he had enjoyed the coffee, but our time together had gone 'too quick' and he felt there were parts of me he 'didnt touch'. Had he been hoping to touch them in Hertfordshire? To be honest, the idea was only 70 per cent appalling. That disgust you feel in your twenties, when all men are repulsive lechers after only one thing, drifts into a more benign attitude in middle age. Perhaps A and B were wrong, and it is possible to be attractive at our stage of life, I thought. I quickly replied to Z saying that I was married and so dinner in Hertfordshire was out of the question. He wrote back in a disappointed way, describing me as a 'nice lady'. I suppose it's the best one can hope for.

June

Z's emails are still coming, despite my polite rebuttal. Sometimes Helllllllllllllo and sometimes Helloooooooooo. He would like to meet again. Sometimes he writes in French or he tries to disguise the emails as work-related, by asking how he can improve his 'writting.' I send dull, polite responses, in the hope that his enthusiasm will peter out.

'We're lucky we're not on the market,' said my friend, over coffee this afternoon. 'On an open market, what do you think we could get? I don't know if we would get anyone, realistically.'

I was offended, of course. I like to think that I could aim high on the market, perhaps net myself an Emeritus Professor, if I frequented the right circles. I've always felt strongly attracted to Emeritus Professors. 'I think we could get someone on the market, depending on where the market is,' I said.

'Tooting Market, maybe,' she said.

Another morning, another workshop. Ten healthcare workers sat ranged around a small windowless room in the basement, waiting while I tried to get my PowerPoint loaded.

'Can anyone . . . ? Does anyone know how to . . . ?' I cast around the room. Usually at this point a man comes forward, presses one button – a button that could never have been guessed at but that, in retrospect, was the obvious button to push – and the thing works. This time nobody stepped forward. I switched it off and switched it on again. I took the memory stick out and put it in again. I looked helplessly around. Finally a woman who had been packing up her things after delivering the previous session came over, connected my laptop to a different port and the overhead screen lit up with my entire Inbox, including the latest missive from Z: 'Heeeeelllllooooooooooo beutifull freind!'

An hour later I felt that I had given my best. My presentation had been lively, with jokes and cartoons, but nobody had laughed or asked any questions. Two of them had even managed to go to sleep, only one deigning to use the thoughtful, hand-on-brow pose. The other just slept, openly.

'It's only half a module,' someone else said cryptically as the group filed out.

Our butcher has always been impatient with customers and now he has become openly abusive. 'All my customers are cunts,' he confided recently.

The other day two or three of us were in the shop when a New Zealander came and asked for lamb shanks. The rest of us froze: we knew how dangerous this was, while she was entirely oblivious, a lamb to the slaughter, you might say. If only we had been able to signal to her.

The butcher's cleaver paused on his block. He looked up from a mess of blood and flesh.

'Do I look like I've got any lamb shanks?' he said.

The woman coloured slightly. 'I don't know. I thought you might . . . ?'

'If you want lamb shanks you'll have to go to WAITROSE.' The woman rushed out blushing, on the verge of tears.

July

I am now regularly in correspondence with Z, although on my side the correspondence consists only of polite requests that he stop writing. I ignore three or four emails in a row – which I notice are now coming from a private account – then send one back, from my work account, acknowledging his good wishes but asking him not to write any more. These sometimes elicit wounded responses about how all he ever wanted was to be friendly. How sad he was, for example, not to be able to call me on his birthday, because I hadn't given him my number. How he doesn't understand what he has done to offend me. How he wishes we could just get together and talk. Other times I get slightly menacing emails, badgering me for my phone number, pressing me to confide my problems in him or reminding me that I owe him for a coffee. He surmises that I am grappling with some deep emotional trauma and need to talk to him about it. I can call him any time, day or night, or he'll come to meet me on his day off. Rationally I know that whatever it is Z wants confers no obligation on to me, but I can't help feeling it does. It's true that he paid for coffee, for instance – does that make me indebted? When someone protests that your behaviour has caused them hurt and bafflement, it's hard not to feel at fault. Emotive language hits home, even when it's baseless.

And now he has written that he is coming to work in my part of the building and 'how funny if we bump on the stairs.' It's strange, considering he works in Compliance that he hasn't realized how non-compliant these missives are.

Looking at old family photograph albums I can't help scanning the pictures for intimations of the disaster that was going to strike us – but my siblings look happy and cheerful, playing in gardens, making sandcastles, laughing like any other children. And it's a woeful kind of archaeology, examining the expressions of people in old photographs for the first signs of alarm, of mental distress. And to all the painful questions – what went wrong? What should have been done differently? – there are no obvious answers.

I have a new desk at the hospital, sitting with a really nice group of managers, mostly in their twenties, always cheerful despite the stresses of their work. Sometimes it feels as though we're all actors in a sitcom about the NHS. People make each other coffee and bring in doughnuts; conversations revolve around bed occupancy and the 'magic money tree'. On Friday at 4 p.m. a dance track goes on to herald the start of the weekend and there's nearly always a birthday to celebrate, or a leaving party, even the odd engagement. Someone brings in cake and we hover among the terminals, levering supermarket sponges into our mouths.

I only have the desk on Fridays. The rest of the time it's used by someone who – judging from the keyboard – suffers from dandruff and a passion for crackers. Even so, I'm protective of this space, however insalubrious, because if I leave it for any length of time, I often find someone else sitting at it when I get back. I won't even go down the corridor to the lavatory if I think there's any danger of someone pinching my seat while I'm gone. Once I was sitting at the desk when a woman I recognized from my previous office came in asking for me. She said someone who worked with her had asked her to find out where I sat. I have a horrible feeling it's Z.

On Twitter today someone posted advice for students applying for a Creative Writing Master of Fine Arts degree.

@Protect your heart. A lot of this shit is luck. Selection is SO subjective. When I applied, I was desperate. Got rejections, got into dream mfa, cuz talent & luck. Don't give applications too much power. Protect your heart. Good luck.

@Also, try going to therapy. Anyone applying to MFA would prob benefit from therapy. Imho getting to understand your own story through therapy will make you better writer.

Then someone replied:

@what the fuck is an MFA

Today I had a meeting in a flash new office with full conferencing facilities to discuss the writing of internal communications. A woman from HR swooshed across the room in high heels and a power suit and dropped a sheaf of documents onto the table in front of me: Storytelling for Team Building.

'Story is key,' she explained, as though this might be news to me. 'We must teach our staff how to tell a story.'

I used to talk about narrative only to people on creative writing courses, or to fellow writers who wanted to debate the merits of the free indirect style. But the art of telling stories has moved into corporate life in a big way. Nowadays business executives in Italian suits keep telling me about the importance of stories.

What changed? Research has shown that listening to stories helps consumers become more empathic and so more likely to buy a product to which the story can be attached. Paul J. Zak, a 'neuroeconomist', has studied the brains of people as they watch a James Bond film and observed 'an amazing neural ballet in which a story line changes the activity of people's brains.' Character-driven stories cause the brain to produce oxytocin and the more oxytocin is produced, the greater a person's ability to empathize with a person or cause – and then to back their empathy with money.

It's the reason why every company now has to have both a 'story' and a 'founding myth'. It's not enough for an artisan bakery to provide very good bread, we need to know how and why two brothers set off on a quest for the perfect loaf. We need to see photographs of the bearded bakers and hear about their journey, their childhood, the sense of epiphany when they suddenly realized that making great bread came down to one thing: the right flour. Their epiphany is our dopamine hit. And dopamine makes you feel good, maybe even good enough to buy an apron, a mug or a canvas shopper, as well as the loaf of bread you originally came in for.

The woman from HR asked if I could devise a workshop on using story to improve communication skills. I said I thought I could.

August

Tacita Dean's exhibition at the Royal Academy includes an hour-long film called *Antigone*. Split screens run concurrent images showing a figure portraying Oedipus roaming in a wild landscape alongside the poet Anne Carson reading from her poem *TV Men: Antigone (Scripts 1 and 2)*.

People coming in and out of the room looked serious as they groped in the darkness for somewhere to sit, inevitably groping parts of other people then furiously apologizing before identifying an empty seat and sitting down with relief. Perhaps soon afterwards these art lovers began wondering when it might be decent to leave again, mentally plotting an exit route with the lowest risk of inappropriate touching.

Back home I took Richard's copy of *Antigone* from the bookcase. He must have studied it for A-level too although he wrote very little in his edition, while mine has notes scrawled on every page. I was experimenting with new handwriting styles the year I turned sixteen, including a Greek kind of e and a French kind of r, and was happy for any excuse to write REALLY SIGNIFICANT in a margin. Some of these really significant bits are even underlined:

Dans la tragédie on est tranquille. D'abord, on est entre soi.

I look through Richard's old books for clues to the person he was, but the tiny, compact handwriting is hard to decipher and doesn't reveal much beyond, say, mixed feelings about T. S. Eliot. Recently I've been reading his copy of Al Alvarez's _The Savage God: A Study of Suicide_. It took me years to gather the courage – I was so frightened of finding a line that seemed to explain why he killed himself, or worse that might, in retrospect, look like a prompt. In fact only one sentence is faintly marked in pencil:

Even the most stoical Romans committed suicide only as a last resort; they at least waited until their lives had become intolerable.

Today I was on my way to the canteen at lunchtime when I spotted Z at the end of the corridor and spun on my heel, walking quickly back to the stairs and then running up them to the eighth floor. It may be the first time I've ever spun on my heel – I think I've only read the phrase before. You don't appreciate what a useful manoeuvre this is until you need to perform it: a 180-degree turn, in half a second. Slippery soles are required, of course – it couldn't be done in trainers. Back at my desk I thought how stupid this was, a woman of my age not able to walk past a person who has been, at worst, a nuisance. I could have taken the opportunity to speak to him in a friendly but firm manner instead of running away like a fifteen-year-old. On the other hand it was exhilarating to feel fifteen again as I legged it up the stairs. I hoped Z hadn't seen me but within minutes I had an email from him assuring me that he had and felt hurt and confused. 'Maybe you didnt see me but I think you did.'

When I came into work today someone was sitting at my desk, someone I had never seen before, surrounded by all the paraphernalia of a loving, working mum: a mousepad with a picture of her children, a lunch box, several pot plants and even a mug that said 'Best Mum Ever'. It was almost a parody of mumness. You might think it would take a few months to make a desk space look that lived in, yet the whole caboodle has landed almost over-night: insta-desk. Even the dandruff-encrusted keyboard now looks sparkly. For all I know, this woman arrived with a box of stuff from some other part of the hospital and assembled it in minutes, while I was down the corridor in the loo. Meanwhile there's no trace of the two managers who used to sit next to me at this end of the office. Where could they have gone? Surely they hadn't been fired? It's as if the old world – the Friday afternoon cakes, the dance track and banter – never existed at all.

107

The new woman looked up and smiled at me. 'Hello – can I help?'

'Hello,' I said. 'I'm the Writing Skills person. I usually sit here on Fridays.'

'Oh,' said the woman, furrowing her brow. 'I've definitely been told that I should sit here from now on. Shall we check with someone?'

I told her not to worry and said it was fine. I would find somewhere else to sit.

Anne Carson talks of translation as being a way to understand people and their histories 'as if we are all separate languages.' I'm interested in her ideas, not just because I am also a translator but because Carson lost her brother too. In her case 'lost' is not a euphemism. Her brother ran away from home in his teens in 1979 and roamed the world under different passports before settling in Copenhagen. Twenty-two years after they had last met he called Carson and said he would like to be reunited. They arranged a meeting but a week before she was due to travel she got a phone call to say that he was dead. Since then she has been trying to decipher or 'translate' him through the things he left behind.

I've often imagined that my brother was travelling somewhere and would one day call home. In Carson's case that really happened. All those years of not knowing where he was must have caused her anguish, and yet I can't help but envy her, however selfish that sounds. He called her in the end.

September

I had an email from someone in Organizational Development who has heard about my 'fabulous skillset' and today we met to talk about planning a series of workshops.

'How are you?' he asked. We were sitting in a 'break-out' area, in deep nourishing sofas that are intended to cradle fragile personalities. People come here to make difficult phone calls, and sometimes to get fired.

'I'm well, thanks.'

'But how are you *really?*' he said, looking at me so intently that I found tears pricking my eyes. I wondered if I should tell him about Z, about losing my desk, about how I currently have to conduct my sessions in the canteen, listening to the same music on a loop. Before I could say any of this, he added.

'I've just been on a course where we were told always to ask twice. Good, isn't it?'

I dreamt that I was helping King Charles collect eggs from the chickens on the Duchy estate. I was putting mine in an old-fashioned wicker basket, while he was tenderly gathering his in the folds of his kilt.

An email from Z: he has got another job and will soon be leaving the hospital. I wrote back wishing him well.

Thank God for that.

It's still warm and the strap marks I got from lying on the beach in San Sebastián last month have barely faded. I may be the only person from that beach to have strap marks since almost everyone else was topless. Every summer I go through the same quandary wondering if it is permissible for someone of my age to wear a bikini, and decide it isn't. This year, feeling emboldened, I walked into a local lingerie shop with the aim of trying on bikinis. This boutique is run by a large, strict German manager, a severe presence amid all the lacey frippery. She's even more frightening than the butcher who calls you a cunt if you ask for lamb shanks.

'Hello!' she barked, as I stood at the door.

'I'm thinking of buying a bikini,' I said. In retrospect I should have been more assertive: I *want* a bikini.

'A what?' Her eyebrows shot so far up her forehead I wondered if they'd ever come down. Lots of women who work in lingerie shops can't perform that manoeuvre any more.

'A bikini,' I said, then faltering, 'Or maybe a tankini?'

'No,' she said, shaking her head, and I was too ashamed to challenge her or ask what she meant by no. Instead I left the lingerie shop thinking how stupid I was ever to think, to dare to think, I could wear a bikini. Then, when we got to San Sebastián it turned out everyone was either in a bikini or topless. Fat and thin, young and old, even extremely old, one hundred plus with tired old bosoms flopped out on their rib cages like hankies drying in the sun. And there I was, in my skirted bathing suit, the most over-dressed woman ever to tread the beach at San Sebastián.

October

Sorting through papers I found an old letter from my penpal Julie:

Hello Panda, How are you? I am fine. My family are all fine. I hope your family are all fine. My teacher Mr Ruden always keeps us in after 3:00 and I hate him. I saw *Staying Alive* and it's got bare ladies in it!!! The Crown Jewels sound really interesting.

And I found a school report of Richard's from when he must have been about sixteen. The teacher, unusually candid by today's standards, wrote that Richard was intelligent but chaotic. That he was destined for triumph or disaster.

Today I saw a white Jaguar pull up on Bond Street and out stepped a young man with bleached hair dressed in a white outfit and carrying a little white dog. An amazing sight, but not useful material for a writer because the picture was already complete – there was nothing I could have added to it.

November

B says that eyebrow-shaping is the most rejuvenating thing a woman can do to her face. She was so shocked to hear that I don't regularly get mine shaped that I felt appalled by my own low standards. At the entrance to Clapham Junction railway station, women lie on a medical bed, practically in the middle of the concourse, clawing at their own cheeks to offer a useful counter-pull while a beautician attacks their facial hair with a piece of thread, one end of which is gripped between her fingers and the other clamped between her teeth. These women lie there, crying and twitching, while hundreds, thousands of commuters swing by, casually taking in the soles of their shoes, which sometimes still have the price tag on them, and the hilly landscape of their bodies beyond them. People queue for the service, too. How does it happen that a woman gets her eyebrows shaped on the way to catch a train? Did she catch sight of herself in the shop window and think 'I need to sort those out right now and I don't care who sees me doing it'? Once or twice I have been at the other end of the thread, with the beautician's teeth bared at me and my fingers straining to make my brow taut. I couldn't make a habit of it.

It's possible that we inherit our approach to make-up. My mother was against excessive grooming. Powder and lipstick from Boots were as far as she would go.

My grandmother, on the other hand, used to remove her eyebrows completely and pencil on two arcs that gave her an appearance of constant surprise. She lived in the north and we lived in the south. Once or twice a year my mother took me up to see her. I was allowed to put the back seat down and make a den in the back of the car with books, toys and a pile of snacks. This was in the days before Jimmy Savile's campaign to make us wear seat-belts, before people knew how safe they were and how dangerous Jimmy Savile was. I reimagined the back of our Simca as a studio flat, like the ones that American sitcoms were set in. We were big fans of *Rhoda* and I knew that Rhoda had an apartment in Manhattan, but I didn't know where Manhattan was, only that there was a pop group called Manhattan Transfer. Once I got to bring a friend with me, but she had never heard of Manhattan either, only Manhattan Transfer.

I n the changing room at the lido today, a naked woman kept talking to me about the joys of cold-water swimming, how hard it was to get in, especially on winter days, but how invigorating it was, how it set you up for the day. And all I really wanted was to know why *T. C. 3/3/95* was inked on her left breast. Over her heart. But also, on the intimate skin of her breast. Did it commemorate a birth, a death of someone? I thought about the way people tell their stories on their bodies, for instance the Mexican builder who once worked at our house and had a whole family saga – portraits of parents and grandparents, names and dates – all on one very muscular arm. Perhaps this woman had found a way to prevent the sad things that happen to us turning into secrets, then percolating through the subconscious and causing havoc in the dangerous territory of memory. The trick might be to proclaim your story, rather than hide it.

December

We went to a party at D's and I got talking to a woman who told me she had been in banking for fifteen years then had a breakdown – she literally collapsed in the street. Her breakdown was so complete, she said, that she couldn't work out how to pick up a cup. She didn't know 'what a light switch was for.' This woman had spent several months in a clinic recovering, and now she was rebuilding her life and expected to return to work, though not to the City. She said that in retrospect she was grateful for a chance to reset the dial. She appeared perfectly composed and contented, although you never know what's going on beneath the surface. Perhaps the greater the composure, the more reason to worry.

Even so, I was entranced by the woman's story. To lose your sense of everything, to have to relearn *everything*, even how to use a cup, sounds like a rare opportunity to start from scratch, to grasp the workings of the world in a way we never get as adults, because we have been picking this stuff up since babyhood. There was something intoxicating about the idea. The blank sheet. The woman didn't seem to have found her ordeal frightening, but perhaps she was still on a lot of medication.

D's grown-up son H was visiting. I haven't seen him for ages and we sat together on the sofa for a while, chatting about what we were up to. For some reason I ended up telling H about the most recent residential writing course

I had taught. There had been a man on the course who wanted to write a memoir about his life as a bodyguard. His career had been exciting, with some celebrity gossip and a few dangerous scrapes, but his writing was dull and he couldn't even make the exciting bits grip. I explained the problem to H, saying I thought this experience could be turned into a marketable book if someone else wrote it for him. There was no particular reason to tell H about this, except as an illustration of the fact that even a really good story can die on the page. I often keep recent students in mind and mention them to other people, in case some useful piece of information or advice comes up that I can pass back to them.

'You could ask RM,' said H.

'RM?'

'Yes, he's a good friend. I've known him for years. He's a journalist but he's done some ghost writing, I think. He lives near me in Sussex. I see him all the time, so I can put you in touch if it's helpful.'

'OK, thanks, I'll think about it,' I said. And I did think about it, a lot, that night and the next day, not because I was selflessly dedicated to the task of finding a ghost writer for my student, but because the name H had mentioned was the same as the name of my brother's best friend at the time of his death, the last person to speak to him, to see him alive. Could it be the same person?

DAY THREE HANDOUT

Reality is what I make it. That is what I have said I believed. Then I look at the hell I am wallowing in, nerves paralyzed, action nullified – fear, envy, hate: all the corrosive emotions of insecurity biting away at my sensitive guts. Time, experience: the colossal wave, sweeping tidal over me, drowning, drowning. How can I ever find that permanence, that continuity with past and future, that communication with other human beings that I crave? Can I ever honestly accept an artificial imposed solution? How can I justify, how can I rationalize the rest of my life away?

SYLVIA PLATH, *The Unabridged Journals*

Day Three

Writing School

S am sat, facing away from the group, arms crossed, shoulders hunched, head bowed. The others all stared at him, puzzled but quiet, some of them taking notes.

We were calling this a Life Class, except that the group had to describe the various positions we asked our models to strike in words, rather than with pencils or pastels. I reckoned writers had as much to learn working from a life model as artists did. They too should sit in circles studying the human form, both naked and clothed, striking different poses – belligerent, languid, apprehensive – and consider the particular set of a jaw, the tension in different muscle groups, the scars and skin folds, in a quest for new and truthful ways to describe a person. We would learn more about people if we looked at their bodies as much as their faces, and considered how they move, stand or sit. Even when we do really look, though, we miss things. Or we see things but don't understand them until, decades later, the truth reveals itself.

In his late teens, Richard had badly burned the back of his hand. I remember the day it happened because I was in the car when my mother took him off to get the injury treated. She explained that he had fallen asleep with his hand against the electric heater in his room. Understandably she was very worried, but I picked up some other tension in the car too, annoyance or fear. I was about nine and remember thinking that it was odd to sleep through such an injury. I couldn't imagine anything like that happening to me. Even so, I accepted this version of events without question and it was only decades later – recently in fact – that I realized Richard must deliberately have burned his hand. What caused me to see the truth, so long afterwards? How does a mind so used to thinking the same, familiar things one day send signals down a different neural pathway? Self-harm is much more talked about now than it was then, so that must be part of the explanation. It would also never have crossed my mind that my mother might lie. But I had a sense, too, of different aspects of my brother's life being revealed to me, like fragments floating to a surface. Ideas and images, obscured for decades, were coming into the light.

Last night's acting games had revealed untapped potential in the group. Peter and Nick had been amusing angels alongside Susie and Jules as demons. Sheena had made a surprisingly comic Bertie Wooster. *Five Children and It* proved a challenge because, while five of us had cavorted about convincingly like children, Diana found it hard to encapsulate 'It'. We had all drunk and laughed a lot. Somebody even said, 'I haven't laughed like this for years.'

In the night, I woke up, heart pounding from drinking too much red wine, with the word Christieland at the front of my mind. I had seen P. D. James use it as shorthand for the classic elements of an Agatha Christie novel. Were we in Christieland, right now, in this country house? There was a would-be spy, a wronged woman, a retired bureaucrat, several carefree youths. One of us had already been the victim of a murder attempt and one had expressed an interest in murder. For Christ's sake, we had *played charades*. At least there was no vicar. I lay very still for a time trying to read into the noises of the old house intimations of danger. A creak came from the corridor and I glanced over at my door where a chair was wedged under the handle. I had put it there before going to sleep, in a fit of paranoia about Nick. My high-vis jacket, hanging on a hook above it was a reminder of the responsibility to stay sober at night. In the event of an emergency I was personally charged with rescuing Sheena – we had even practised this scenario on the first day. She had shown me where she kept her dressing gown and slippers, her walking stick and hearing aid. I shouldn't have drunk so much. Jesus. My head was killing me. I took some paracetamol and eventually managed to get back to sleep, but by the time I woke up it was too late to go for a run, never mind enjoy a solitary breakfast.

'How's it going?' Tom asked the group, as they frowned over their notebooks, looking at Sam. 'Have you finished your paragraphs?'

'It's making me realize how much harder it is to describe someone when you can't see their face,' said Susie, obligingly. Perhaps it was this willingness to serve up the required response that had driven Susie's husband into the arms of her best friend, I thought, and I wondered how that woman felt about everything now. Was she horrified by the extent of her betrayal, by Susie's devastation or was she still sure that it had been right to start a relationship with a man who was twenty-five years into a marriage and might have appeared to be on the home stretch? She must have been so sure they were right for each other – or perhaps she was going through her own crisis. Knowing she ran a stables, I couldn't help picturing this woman in jodhpurs and with a riding crop.

Susie had been a bride in one of last night's literary charades, with a tablecloth we found in a drawer in the kitchen serving as her veil. By then the centre directors and other staff had gone back to their own homes and we tutors were left in charge. Somebody took a sheet of A4 from the office and cut a frame out of it which Susie held around her face. Sam had 'visited' her, as she sat primly on the sofa, left the room, then visited her again. The rest of us in this team had thought the title would be guessed too easily but in fact Sam had to come through the door several times, each time with more panache, sometimes bowing deeply, sometimes skidding towards Susie on bended knee, before the other team got *Brideshead Revisited*. By the time of his last entrance, when he landed on Susie's lap, she had been weeping with laughter.

'Bet you're glad you stayed now, aren't you?' I asked her, when our paths crossed in the kitchen.

'Definitely,' she said and held up a bottle of wine. 'Plus this helps. Who needs men, right? Fuck 'em.' The unaccustomed expletive seemed to unsteady her and she righted herself against the door frame as she returned to the sitting room, bangles tinkling.

After the game we stayed talking in the sitting room and, sometime around midnight, those of us still downstairs moved into the kitchen and started investigating the fridges.

'Who actually drinks this stuff?' said Jim, holding up a carton of oat milk.

'Lynn, I think,' said Kisi, exchanging a look with Zoe. She was making hot chocolate for everyone while Sam prepared bacon and eggs.

'Where was Lynn tonight?' Zoe asked.

'She's gone home,' said Tom. 'Decided it wasn't for her.' I wanted to mention Lynn's complaint about the lack of 'fun activities' and get a bigger audience for my waterslide joke but instead I followed Tom's diplomatic lead, offering merely a sad smile.

'O–K,' said Sam in a drawn out way that suggested he had plenty to say about that, but would keep his counsel.

'And Lily?'

'She's gone to bed,' said Jules.

'She told me she wanted to get on with some writing,' said Kisi. The ambivalent set of her mouth, one corner sucked against her teeth, expressed something the rest of us may have been thinking: that Lily was taking her writing a little too seriously. She had gone upstairs to work while the rest of us drank and messed around downstairs. Perhaps she was journalling.

'Important to let your hair down,' said Zoe with a small but decisive nod and there was a surge of agreement around the table as Jim uncorked another bottle.

Some time between 12.30 and 1 a.m., I experienced that rocketing love that comes with an alcoholic launch pad, along with a profound revelation – fuzzily defined but something to do with the healing power of groups. There were Sam and Zoe at the oven, plating up eggs and bacon, while Kisi whipped cream for the hot chocolates. Nick was talking to Jules and Jim about the ways in which Eastbourne had changed since he was a child, and they looked genuinely interested. Diana had gone off to bed, blowing us a flurry of kisses from the doorway with her elbows held high in a parody of stardom. It took some nerve to come and live with a bunch of strangers for five days, I thought, especially if you were an introvert, and it really was hard to read your writing aloud in front of other people – harder perhaps than I allowed for when I was leading a workshop. I never read my own work aloud, after all. I was far too secretive, too superstitious. Perhaps I wouldn't be brave enough. Groups could be daunting, even frightening, but so often they proved to be a source of kindness and mutual support. Love had washed over me.

Looking round the table this morning, it was hard to tell how much of this had been revealed. I hoped I hadn't hugged or told anyone I loved them. That wouldn't look good on the feedback form. They all seemed absorbed in their descriptions of Sam's begrudging back view, taking it in turns to read out their passages and listening intently to the others as they read.

'I think what we've seen here is that it's important not to focus too hard on people's facial expressions,' said Tom. 'Their bodies say as much, or maybe more, than their faces. Or they may say something *different*.' He paused, marking this paradox for the upturned faces. 'A person might be smiling, but you can see from the way they hold themselves that they're angry, in which case the body may be a more trustworthy guide to a person's character or state of mind than their face. There's an interesting tension, there. Something to think about anyway.'

He introduced the next exercise, which was to use the observations everyone had made during the Life Class to start a short story about a character, then to outline how that story would continue, just as William Trevor's description of Leary builds into a tale of manipulation and the deception of two widowed sisters. 'You've got forty minutes,' he called. 'Get creative!'

In the kitchen I flicked on one of the kettles, then looked out of the window, watching the younger members of the group gather at their habitual spot outside. It was good to see Lily at the heart of things, laughing and smiling with the others. Meanwhile, Peter was advancing steadily into my peripheral vision.

'Good gracious!' he exclaimed, pausing at the island, 'has someone been baking?'

'Chocolate muffins – amazing, aren't they?' I said. 'We certainly won't starve! Can I make you a coffee to help with the writing exercise, or are you already inspired enough?'

'No thank you, and I'm afraid I won't be doing the exercise. I find myself somewhat resistant to these writing prompts.' The word 'resistant' popped out of him, like unexpected wind.

'Fair enough.' I decided to be charitable. 'I know what you mean. It's difficult to be creative on demand. Not something one can switch on and off.'

'Well, interesting you should say that,' said Peter, propping himself against the counter with the air of someone who plans to hold forth. 'Perhaps we can. On the train up I was reading about the fascinating advances in computer creativity. I don't think it will be long before we see a computer scooping the top fiction prize.'

'Yes, they say that, don't they.' The kettle reached its own maximum expression and quietly disengaged. I banged a few cupboard doors open and shut before finding a cafetière, then shook coffee into it and poured over the water. 'Isn't this just another version of the infinite monkeys bashing out Shakespeare, though? Surely we don't believe that a computer's going to write *Middlemarch*, or *Great Expectations*.'

Susie, Diana and Jules had come into the kitchen and were cooing over the muffins. Sam had switched on the other kettles and was lining up mugs for the group outside.

'No', said Peter, 'it's entirely different, because there's nothing random about artificial intelligence. In time, given the right data, computers will match our potential and overtake it. Machine learning is leading us in that direction.'

'Dreadful thought,' said Susie, shuddering.

'There's really no reason why it should be!' said Peter, with an exasperated laugh.

I forced the plunger down, splattering coffee onto the counter. 'Shit.' I remembered that Borges character, Pierre Menard, who sets out to write an identical version of *Don Quixote* without re-reading the original, as an experiment to see if it is possible to ride the same creative streak more than once.

'Here,' said Sam, handing over kitchen towel with the efficiency of a theatre nurse.

'Thanks. But a human mind *conceived* those stories, Peter. The miracle is in the conception.' I was surprised to hear myself sounding so religious. 'Do you really think a machine, which has no concept of love, or grief or suffering, can write about those uniquely human experiences? Even if the exercise was convincing, it would be in bad faith.'

'People are all different, Peter,' added Jules, soothingly, 'how can a computer capture all our wonderful variations?'

'Computers are already capturing them. Creativity is just a process, like any other. You don't have to be human, you just have to master the process. It's been proven.'

'Well then frankly what are we doing here? That's it for human creativity,' I said brightly, picking up a muffin. 'We're stuffed. There's really no point in being a person.'

'None at all,' said Diana, 'Much better to be a dog.'

I took my coffee outside and sat down next to Tom with a theatrical sigh.

'What news from yonder?'

'Nothing really. We're about to be replaced by robots.'

'Sounds good. How soon can they get here?'

Creativity wasn't always recommended for the aspiring writer. In the nineteenth century literature students were encouraged to emulate canonic writers and not to think their own offerings could stand comparison with the greats. It may have been Barrett Wendell, a Harvard Professor, who first introduced a creative element into the proceedings in the early 1900s, when he started setting his students a daily exercise in which to write one hundred words in a 'fluent and agreeable style' about something they had observed during the day. Wendell's writing exercise was mocked by some critics, but 'the daily theme' proved popular, and soon it was being prescribed in other universities and colleges. At Wellesley College, poet Katherine Lee Bates found it a useful tool 'to quicken observation and give as much practice as possible in the sifting and grouping of facts of personal experience.' By the 1930s Virginia Woolf was referring to herself as 'a creative writer' in her diary.

This 'creative' approach spread from universities to schools, where children were encouraged to let their imaginations roam unfettered, an ethos that still prevails in primary schools. My own children used to write wildly imaginative stories for homework (admittedly with the conventional opening 'It all began when') and they were taught never to settle for a pedestrian word like 'said'. So the characters in their stories shouted and exclaimed, sobbed, gasped and shrieked. Later they bellowed, declared and insisted, and had the experiment continued they might by now be abjuring and expostulating – but thankfully, regular writers soon learn that the best option is, after all, nearly always 'said.'

Can we really be taught creativity? It makes financial sense for cash-strapped humanities faculties to believe we can. An inspiring teacher may make all the difference to a writer and some of their methods have passed into literary legend. At Boston University in the 1950s Robert Lowell might treat his students – who included Sylvia Plath and Anne Sexton – to three hours on one line of Blake. Jay McInerney recalled fifteen minutes debating one word, 'earth', with his teacher Raymond Carver at Syracuse in the 1980s. These days, at Syracuse, there are 7,000 applications for six places. How is it possible to place six aspiring writers above 6,994 others?

Yet writing courses keep proliferating, giving thousands of students the opportunity to pay serious attention to the craft of making stories. Meanwhile the teacher–writers get a steady income and a reason to brush their hair and leave the house. The experience can be as invigorating for them as for the students. 'Giving workshops to people who can't write yet, while we can't write yet either, is a traditional way for nascent writers to earn their crusts,' says A. L. Kennedy in *On Writing*, but she also identifies a creeping aggrandisement in the creative writing world. What began as a 'workshop' became a 'masterclass', with a price tag to match. Similarly, what was once an interesting opportunity – a forum for writing and talking about words – began to feel like a requirement, like 'professional development'. A pressure grew to get training, to take an expensive degree, especially once word got out that agents and publishers prioritized manuscripts from Creative Writing graduates. Was this a closed shop? To writers it seemed as though you might need a qualification to have any hope of getting published.

Fashions change, of course. Rumours went round that too many writers had studied their craft, that publishers were looking for something less polished. A couple of dazzling successes from the slush pile tilted the balance back in favour of the unschooled writer. Some critics said they could detect a similarity in the writing of MFA graduates. In 2016 language professors Andrew Piper and Richard Jean So tried to quantify this difference through machine learning. They marshalled their data analysis tools and found ... nothing. There was no discernible variation in style, vocabulary or subject matter between the novels of writers who had studied creative writing at one of twenty top American institutions and those who hadn't studied it at all, although the professors noted that writers with an MFA were more likely to use the words 'lawn', 'lake', 'counter', 'stomach', and 'wrist' and to call their characters Ruth, Pete, Bobby, Charlotte, and Pearl. Writers without an MFA showed a slight preference for Anna, Tom, John, and Bill.

Was that all it boiled down to? Ruth over Anna? Bobby over John? The professors also discovered that 96 per cent of MFA novels feature mainly male characters while that figure was 99 per cent in the non-MFA group and that, in both cases, 'the contemporary American novel is dispropor- tionately preoccupied with the experiences of men'. They concluded that there was no tangible difference between the schooled and the unschooled writer, and that $200 million, the amount spent yearly on MFAs, was 'a high price to pay for very little measurable impact'.

For thousands of students, the real value of a course is in the regular contact with fellow writers who under- stand what they are trying to do and can make useful contributions. It's hard enough to guarantee that alchemy will occur in a creative writing group, let alone put a price on it.

'Can I ask a question?' Lily said, after we had returned from our break and listened to everyone read. It was so rare to hear from her that even a question about asking a question was welcome.

'Go ahead,' said Tom.

'Do you always carry a notebook?'

'I think it's a good idea,' said Tom, 'if you can remember.'

'I keep a pad and pencil by the bog', said Jules, on a raspberry-scented exhalation that made this seem like a beautiful thing to do.

'And ideally have another one by the bed,' I said.

Flashes of inspiration often occurred, I explained, in that time when consciousness begins to melt towards sleep. Sometimes the flashes were so bright that I persuaded myself there was no need to put on the light and grope for a notebook; the image, or idea was so brilliant it was bound to be there in the morning. It never was, of course. You had to capture the idea and etherize it, like Nabokov with his butterflies.

'What did everyone think about the Plath extract on today's handout? Tom asked. 'Do you think it's truthful? Is she writing for herself, or posterity?'

'It's so painful,' Kisi said, sadly shaking her head. 'I don't see how it could be anything but truthful.'

'But isn't that because you know what happened to her?' Jules said. 'If her life had turned out more happily then you would look at this and think it's just another adolescent diary.'

'An extremely tormented adolescent,' said Diana. 'The 'colossal wave', sweeping tidal over me, drowning, drowning.'

'Well they generally are tormented,' said Jules.

'Much depends on whether or not she thought this would be published,' said Diana.

'Does knowing that something might be published alter its integrity?' I asked.

'It has to,' said Jim. 'You're bound to be more careful about what you say, because you don't want to hurt people.'

'But then that means the diary is a performance and it can't really be honest.'

'Isn't all life, or much of it, a performance?' said Diana. 'I don't see any reason to behave differently on paper.'

Last night for their charade on *Warrior Queens*, she had persuaded Peter to wield his stick like a samurai sword, then to mince about the room like Quentin Crisp. Then, acting out the full title, she had ridden into the room astride Sam and Nick, as Boudicca. None of us got the title, but we were all mesmerized by the show.

'Let's say you know for sure your diaries will be burned after you die,' I said. 'Could you be completely honest then?'

'Not a hundred per cent,' Kisi said, 'Someone can still read it while you're alive. I don't know how you get past that.'

'Hide it,' said Zoe.

'There's nowhere my mum wouldn't look,' said Kisi. 'Swear to God.'

'I have a full collection of appointment diaries going back fifty years,' said Peter, clasping his hands in front of him, managerial style. 'I can find out exactly what I was doing on any given day from the 1970s onwards.'

'Peter knows where the bodies are buried,' Sam laughed.

'I'm sure that's useful, Peter, but it's not the same as a journal. What about your *feelings*? How do you remember what you *felt*?' Jules asked.

'Oh I don't have any feelings,' Peter said with a quick, childish shrug. 'None I would consider worth recording, anyway. What would be the point?'

What was the point of any of it, you might think. Being a writer requires an arsenal of conflicting qualities – a supreme self-belief married to humility, a determination to succeed together with the strength to deal with failure. You have to aim high because the middle distance is too pointless, too fuzzy a goal. You have to want success more than anything (John Cheever dreamed of his face on a stamp) while accepting that it isn't that big a deal if you don't get it. The legion of once-rejected authors parades before us: J. K. Rowling, Sarah Waters, James Joyce. In 1797 *Pride and Prejudice* was 'declined by Return of Post' by publisher Thomas Cadell, and Jane Austen waited another sixteen years before finding a publisher. It's sold 20 million copies since then. My own father's rejected manuscript on the development of selfhood in children used to lie for days on the doormat before he stooped to pick it up. Rejection is built into the experience of writing. But almost worse than the stories of rejection are the ones about wasted time. The people who spend years, decades, on a book that may never be read, or be quickly remaindered, or sold for resurfacing roads.

We keep writing, all the same, driven by the desire to tell a story and perhaps in the process to understand something about ourselves. We're the descendants of Freud, after all, and we watch a lot of detective dramas, spend our evenings admiring Scandinavian or Italian or Scottish landscapes as brilliant but troubled sleuths stir their coffee in a Midlands kitchen or grimly sink a pint in an Oxfordshire pub, or swing thoughtfully in Caribbean hammocks, or stare stonily into shallow graves in the Shetlands, or walk frowning into abattoirs in Stockholm, or stalk through the snow in Canada. Always frowning, always thinking. We want to apply that same troubled genius to the people and events of our own lives.

Some of the people who came to the writing school hoped to address a grievance or to salve a hurt and, as they told their story, *their truth*, during the course of the week it could seem that the grievance – often concerning a less than perfect parent – was disproportionate to the crime. That need to be understood and validated, to tell 'my truth' rarely made for good writing. You have to write for yourself, not to make a point. Perhaps it was too much to ask, the imperative to be 'creative', to look inwards and draw the story out, instead of looking out at what was already there.

After lunch I walked into the kitchen, heading for the kettle, and found Jules and Sheena facing me, Diana behind them at the sink.

'We can always tell when you're coming,' said Jules. 'From the tappity tap of your shoes on the tiles.'

Sheena and Diana smiled in recognition of this trait of mine. 'Tappity tap tap,' Diana said, as she opened the fridge to take out some milk.

I looked down at my leather-soled shoes. Tappity tap was far from the image I hoped to project. I preferred to think of myself as a stylish bluestocking, bookish but glamorous.

'Oh look she's gone all self-conscious!,' said Jules, stepping forward and ruffling my hair.

'Not at all!' I protested, self-consciously. 'I'm just sorry I can't sneak up on you!'

But as I walked carefully away with my coffee, I wondered if I lacked the gravitas, or star quality required in a creative-writing teacher. Perhaps my students saw me more as a mascot. At lunch, when I'd helpfully brought water to the table for everyone, Sheena had called out 'Nice jugs!'

Would anyone shout 'nice jugs' to Marilynne Robinson? Would Vladimir Nabokov have stood for such familiarity when he was teaching Russian literature at Cornell in the 1950s? His lectures habitually drew crowds, not least because they became a double-act. His wife Vera, sitting in the front row, might be called upon to change slides, alter the lighting or draw an impromptu sketch of Emma Bovary on the blackboard. Nobody would have ruffled Nabokov's hair, I thought, even if he had had any hair to ruffle.

Nabokov told his students that great writing should make us not think, but *shiver*.

I have tried to teach you to read books for the sake of their form, their visions, their art. I have tried to teach you to feel a shiver of artistic satisfaction, to share not the emotions of the people in the book but the emotions of its author – the joys and difficulties of creation.

I knew what he meant by that, the moment when, through a particular combination of form and content, a writer recasts some area of experience such that the reader sees it as if for the first time. Something new is said about the world and what it is to be human. Evelyn Waugh called this 'experience totally transformed.' There are writers who deliver regular shivers; Zora Neale Hurston, for example, in *Their Eyes Were Watching God*. Alan Hollinghurst or Alice Munro can both make you shiver as, through their eyes, you see life differently.

Writers feel that shiver, too, when they know they have hit the mark, when a phrase or sentence rises above the sum of its parts to express something new. The writer succeeds in articulating some elusive concept and delivering the result straight to the most receptive part of the reader's brain. At the start of a project you labour away to make the beast move. You despair, cry on the sofa, eat biscuits. Then a point comes when it seems stronger, lighter, ready to take flight. All your ideas make sense and in fact are coming so fast you have to clutch at surfaces – bits of paper, napkins, envelopes, your own skin – to write them down. The house is full of enigmatic notes. People talk and you try to block out what they are saying so that you can concentrate on a new idea. You feel annoyed with your friends for wanting to meet up and annoyed with your children for wanting to be fed. Students of literature spend hours wondering what an author means by this or that, and seem to locate the writer's skill in the clever display of symbolism and metaphors. But when writing's going well, it's so much better than that. You choose some words to describe a concept or action and the combination somehow produces a different effect, suggesting an idea or a picture you had never thought of before but that you see now is right and true. Gabriel García Márquez compares the experience to levitation. Zadie Smith identifies a kind of 'magical thinking':

Something has changed. And it's not restricted to the house. If you go outside, everything – I mean, *everything* – flows freely into your novel. Someone on the bus says something – it's straight out of your novel. You open the paper – *every single story in the paper is directly relevant to your novel*. If you are fortunate enough to have someone waiting to publish your novel, this is the point at which you phone them in a panic and try to get your publication date brought forward because you cannot believe *how in tune the world is with your unfinished novel right now*, and if it isn't published next Tuesday maybe the moment will pass and you will have to kill yourself.

That sense of startling synchronicity, when everything in life magically responds to the work in progress, is hard to explain without sounding either boring or mad. 'You'll never believe this,' you say, and watch the eyes of people you love glaze over. It may be that such coincidences are happening around us all the time and it takes the heightened state that comes with a book in full flow to reveal them. For a writer, it's like travelling in a new area of consciousness and you miss it when the journey's over.

Lily, the quiet American broker, had made me shiver as I sat reading her stories, and I realized that I had got her wrong on that first evening. Her job in the City and her interest in 'journalling' – with its deadening associations of wellness and self-care – had been enough for me to think she was unlikely to be a good writer. I was wrong. Lily was a very good writer, perhaps the best in the group.

I had found her bundle of papers outside my room and read them over lunch. Her stories were set in the financial worlds of New York and London, her characters young international corporates who spent their days stranded at the top of skyscrapers, gliding past one another in transparent lifts, looking through the glass but too anxious about their careers to make meaningful connections. Their social media showed images of holidays and parties meant to disguise their loneliness. Rarely had I met a cast of characters who seemed both so alien and so endearing. These people's emotions didn't float free but were part of a picture connected to their working life, the details of which, like the factory in *American Pastoral*, were interesting in themselves. The drama of the trading floor, the need to fuel their adrenaline with drugs or with ever greater personal challenges – marathons and mountain-climbing – this felt like new information, told in a new way.

'I think these are great,' I said to Lily, when she came down to the shed.

'Really?' A surprising blush swept over her face, swooping under the border of her fringe.

'Have you shown them to anyone else before?'

'Only my boyfriend. But he's not really ... he doesn't really read books.'

'Well I read books and I've never read anything quite like this. You've taken me into a world I knew nothing about, and that's what fiction's all about. I think you're a terrific writer. It's only my opinion, but—'

'Of course,' Lily nodded quickly. 'I'm not expecting ...'

'But there's no reason why you shouldn't. The world of publishing is unfair, etc. etc., we say it a zillion times – but I think you should show these to an agent.'

'Really? Wow. I'm, I – I—'

'Definitely! I can suggest some names to you if you like.'

138

'I don't know what to say. That would be great, thank you.'

'And there are other options. You know, competitions, magazines. Have you ever tried anything like that?'

'No,' Lily quickly shook her head as if such a thing would be far too presumptuous. 'I wouldn't know where to begin.'

'I can give you some pointers. They would be something to aim for. Sometimes a deadline can be helpful. You know, the imposition of a goal, I suppose. Am I making sense? It's been a long day!'

We laughed at the awkwardness of giving and receiving praise and our laughter bounced off the walls of the byre. A moment of triumph in a cow shed. It was always a pleasure to see the joy of someone who had hoped she was doing something well, and found that there was at least one other person who thought she was.

As Lily walked away I wondered, of course, although I didn't ask, if she was one of the women in those glass lifts, wanting so much to make a connection, but always gliding past the point of contact.

Exercise Three

Writing from Life

The death of someone close requires grasping two distinct facts. First, that the person has died. Second, that you will never see them again. The first of these is made easier by all the sad obligations that accompany a death. A funeral has to be arranged, friends and family informed, notices placed in the paper, the death registered, workplaces contacted, the rented room emptied and its contents brought home. There will be visitors, a hearse, a coffin lowered into a grave, tea and sandwiches. There's no denying death: all the admin confirms it.

The second fact is much harder to absorb. How can it be possible that you will never see this person again? It makes no sense, when their shoes still retain the unmistakable shape of their feet, when there's a yoghurt, bought by them, in the fridge, appointments still in the diary for next week. Isn't the main function of appointments to demonstrate our commitment to staying alive? It feels ridiculous, ringing up to cancel an arrangement because the person who made it has died. It's like the worst excuse, the ultimate in avoidance strategies. 'He can't come to your party because he's dead.' Yeah, right.

After a bereavement, the brain has to make impossible adjustments. It's why the first instinct of so many people, on hearing that someone has died, is to telephone that person, to share with them the news of their own death.

'I had no idea you were so ill!'

'I know, me neither! I thought it was just a bad flu.'

'Were you, I mean, did you not take the right precautions or something?'

'Hang on – are you blaming me for this?'

'No of course not! It's just – well, it's really sad!'

'Tell me about it.'

In dreams my brother often phoned to say that there had been a mistake: he had been in Australia all along, or too busy to check his messages; he hadn't realized everyone was trying to reach him. People talk of expecting to see their loved one walking into the room, as sad and perplexed as everyone else is in the house. It's the magical thinking Joan Didion famously describes in her account of the year following her husband's death. We can't get our heads around death, even though it happens all the time, every day, every minute, with every turn of the second hand. Why can't we get used to this thing that keeps happening to us? Because love is stronger than common sense. Pop songs have been telling us this for years and we didn't take them seriously.

Then there's the grieving 'process'. We all know that it's something we have to 'go through', without, perhaps, understanding exactly what that process is or how long it's supposed to take, how we should go through it. People talk wisely of time healing the pain. They don't say how much pain or how much time.

And while it's true that the pain, in its most visceral sense, doesn't last forever, it's sad to lose that, too. The pain, after all, is a connection to the person who has died. You feel alive when grief is tearing at you. You can do anything, take on anyone. You're Antigone, scrabbling in the dirt, defying the authorities. Then the pain subsides and you shuffle meekly back into the chorus. Maybe forever afterwards you feel less real, because you have done something that ought not to be possible: you have 'got over it', just as people promised you would and you silently vowed you wouldn't. Because it shouldn't be possible to get over the violent death of someone young. It feels like a betrayal.

After his younger brother was drowned, William Wordsworth swore in his poem 'Elegiac Stanzas' that he would never stop grieving for him.

> *Not for a moment could I now behold*
> *A smiling sea, and be what I have been:*
> *The feeling of my loss will ne'er be old;*
> *This, which I know, I speak with mind serene.*

This feeling of my loss will ne'er be old. But it does get old, soften, lose its edge. And as the poet Robert Pack remarked of these lines, 'To commit oneself to endless and undiminished grief, as if that is the only way to remain loyal to the deceased, is surely an unconvincing and perverse form of serenity.' Pack may never have experienced the kind of grief that seems destined never to lift. And, perhaps rather than 'serene', what Wordsworth meant, although it didn't rhyme so well, was 'resolved'.

Like Antigone, I resolved not to disavow my brother in the years after his death. I would keep visiting his grave. I would often talk about him. I would wear his raggedy old jumpers, listen to his records and read his books. In a painful conversation, I asked my mother to keep putting flowers on his grave, something she was reluctant to do. 'I don't believe that's where he is,' she reasoned. But I wanted him to be honoured; I'd had terrible nightmares about a desecrated headstone. I visited his room, still not cleared in the weeks after his death, and sat looking at his sad belongings. Nothing sadder than the possessions of a person who is no longer there to possess them.

It was hard to keep him in the conversation though, especially at home, where it quickly became almost impossible to talk about Richard. Nobody was to blame for that – avoidance was something we learned to do together, collectively steering away from difficult subject matter when we saw it looming on the road ahead. On the rare occasions when that wasn't possible – say a visitor came who didn't know the rules – there was always an option to slip out of the room, or improvise a coughing fit. I used to opt for one or the other before M*A*S*H came on, because I couldn't bear to hear the line 'suicide is painless' in the theme tune. Later I decided that I couldn't listen to R. E. M.'s 'Everybody Hurts', either. I didn't want to hear anything by Nirvana or Tori Amos. I didn't want to read *Jude the Obscure*, or watch *The Wall* or talk about Sylvia Plath. The number of things that couldn't be said or heard multiplied, until it was hard to keep track of them, or remember who was up to speed with the latest protocol.

At home we denied ourselves the chance to talk about someone we had all loved. The few photographs we had of Richard disappeared into drawers. His possessions were redistributed among friends and charity shops, though I managed to salvage some of his books when I realized that my father was tearing out the flyleaf if Richard had written his name there. I don't think he was trying to excise my brother; he just didn't want to risk being blindsided by the sight of his handwriting, such a powerful evocation of character. It must have been particularly sad for my mother, who wanted to remember and talk about the son she had brought into the world. Occasionally she mentioned his name and the air between us froze. How much easier life must be, I thought glibly, for the friend whose brother had died of an illness and was still present in their family home, both in conversations and photographs. They kept him with them, while we seemed to lose my brother all over again, by not acknowledging him. 'The boy is dead,' Tiresias says to Creon in Anne Carson's *Antigonick*, 'stop killing him.' There was something 'cleaner' about a death from illness as opposed to a suicide. For Carson's Ismene the family is 'doubled tripled degraded and dirty in every direction'. I felt that we were like that. I was scared to become a pariah.

There were good reasons not to talk about Richard, not least the fact that my sister herself had developed a devastating mental illness. Perhaps her illness was connected to his death or there was a genetic factor and I could also become ill. I felt fine, though, and that seemed very unfair. Why should both my siblings suffer so terribly and not me? 'We mustn't open old wounds,' my father said. He spoke about Richard only occasionally, usually late at night, until the last year of his life when dementia raced through his mind like Thing One and Thing Two, ripping up conventions and throwing open doors that had long been marked 'Do Not Enter'. Then my father started asking me about Richard every time I visited, and I would have to keep breaking the news of his death. He heard it as though for the first time and would be distraught and ask me for the details, and I had to give them. This felt like a punishment for all the years we hadn't talked about what happened. Other times when I visited, my father would assure me that he had just seen Richard, who was very well and about to start a new business, running a vineyard in France or a farm in Australia, and we would talk about him contentedly, because I enjoyed these reveries as much as he did.

Away from home, I made an effort to keep my brother in the conversation. It was hard to keep mentioning him, though, since that often meant explaining that he was dead and I had promised myself never to lie about the way he died. The determination began to feel like a kind of masochism. Friends who knew about him had to become appropriately sad at the mention of his name. People who didn't had to have the story explained, which was painful. I could avoid it by pretending that he had never existed, but that was unconscionable. I had made a rod for my own back. For one thing, it was – still is – hard to say his name. I got around the problem by mentioning him quickly or quietly, or while my back was turned, or on an exhalation so that people couldn't be sure what they had heard. It felt like a clever linguistic trick, a child's ploy: just because you didn't hear it doesn't mean I didn't say it. These tricks and deflections became second nature. I was a teenager, after all, and didn't want to trail gloom wherever I went, or leave the door open to endless grief.

A little tragedy, on the other hand, could be alluring. At fifteen, an age when all of us want to seem more interesting, it gave me instant drama. The boys I liked hung out in darkened rooms listening to the Cure and helping each other apply black eyeliner and my experience gave me a certain mystique. Young tragedian was a good look, plus I could do my own eyeliner. 'I know it sounds bad, but I wish something really awful would happen to me too,' said one friend as we stood behind 'the shed' at school. This was a designated area for sixth formers to smoke on certain conditions: so long as we kept up a pretence of hiding, the staff pretended not to see us there. I knew what my friend meant. We can turn events to our advantage. Writers are no better than teenagers in that respect. Formative experiences give shape to our books, as well as our lives.

Not long after my brother's funeral, I visited his grave after days of torrential rain and was anguished by the scene. In a letter to a friend that was never sent, I wrote:

> You can almost tell where the coffin is because instead of a mound, which is usual on a grave, there's a dip in the earth, it actually goes down over the coffin and if I had stood on it, it would have collapsed.

I felt, with Antigone, the terrible insult of an improper burial site. 'He's only been dead six weeks and no one can be bothered to put anything decent on the grave.'

I wasn't about to repair the damage – I'm no Greek heroine. Then again Antigone's motivation has itself changed over the two thousand years since Sophocles created her. In Ancient Greece she would have been played by a boy. The tragedy belonged less to her than to Creon, the King, whose hamartia in going against the gods leads to a terrible punishment: the suicides of his wife and son as well as Antigone's. Over time the heroine's psychology changed along with her physique, but the moral tussle was still between what is owed to the gods and to the state. 'Two principles,' wrote George Eliot, 'both having their validity, are at war with each other.'

Twentieth-century interpretations saw her rebellion as more about justice than duty. In Poland she stood for the Solidarity strikers and in Mexico for victims of domestic abuse. In Northern Ireland, she embodied political themes both for Tom Paulin (*The Riot Act*) and Seamus Heaney (*The Burial at Thebes*). Bertolt Brecht, like Anouilh, moved the action to World War II and used Antigone to make a stand against barbarism.

More recently she has become an icon of female rebellion, a symbol for queerness, for difference, for pacifism, climate activism. In every interpretation she stands up to authority in the name of doing what is right and just. Does she *love* her brother, though?

In a version of the play written by Euripides, perhaps twenty years after Sophocles, and later lost, Antigone's fiancé actually helps to bury her brother. Neither of them dies. Instead they marry and have a son. Love wins! How differently we might view Antigone if Euripides' version had been the one to survive, and Sophocles' the one that was lost.

I wanted to keep my love for Richard alive, but protecting a wound is exhausting. Over time the protection becomes more important than the wound itself. You can't keep slipping out of the room whenever somebody mentions suicide or cough all the way through 'Everybody Hurts'. That would be four minutes, forty-six seconds of coughing. As I entered my twenties, the resolve to keep Richard present in my life began to slip. It was easier, by then, to say there had only ever been four of us. We move on and the person we loved, and still love, travels away from us. So much more is forgotten than remembered – the way they moved or spoke, the change in atmosphere when they came into a room, the warmth of their hand, the sound of their footsteps. All that remains of a life cut short is a packet of memories that gets thinner with every passing year.

Richard was a mystery at the centre of my life. His life had greatly affected mine and yet I knew so little about it. The years of silence at home had made me yearn to know more about him. I wished that I could remember more or that I could be brave enough to ask the people who had known him well for their own memories. Sometimes I searched online for the names of his friends and wondered about contacting them, but that felt like a strange, indecent thing to do. I had a photograph of Richard framed, then found I couldn't bring myself to put it up. I didn't want to keep explaining it to people, or feeling sad about what had happened.

And so it went on for thirty years until I got an email from a friend who said he had been sent some poems to review by the writer Adam Thorpe, and that one of them seemed to be about my brother. He forwarded the book to me and there it was, a poem about Richard, dedicated to him by name:

DEFEAT

in memoriam Richard France

With the backdrop of a London caff
we'd feel more real – us preened

and patted, public-school types
plotting subversion in the glory days

(a kind of green-striped red). You remember
the worker, I presume? Powdered with his wage,

weary, he'd smack the butt-end of the ketchup
or cradle the mug like a lover's face,

pouting into steam. Knew all the ropes, we reckoned –
life's block and tackle, that head for heights . . .

the struggle's hoplite, slumped on the eve
of some enormous strife. And if

our last conversation was not in a caff
but somewhere fancy with tubular chairs

and menus so thin, so tall, they couldn't
take the wind from your gestures, still

we were saving the world over breakfast
in the plunge and soar of it: your intellect

seared with passion. Look, Ad, we've
to change our lives for once and for all.

Something removed your retaining wall
in the few short weeks between then and when

you took to the air from a Deptford warehouse
back in '82 – high enough to matter, of course.

Since then, the silence. And no more signals (as far
as I'm concerned) but your brief, unassuming parts

in dreams – like the early roles a film star
might look shyly back on, yet grieve for.

I read the poem. Read it again and again. Standing in the kitchen, holding the book, ready to run out if someone came in. The air was still. Everything went quiet.

This was incendiary. This was contraband. We had made a decision, in my family, not to speak about Richard and here was someone breaking the rules. Thorpe was not only speaking about my brother but publishing details of his death that not even close friends of ours knew. My hands shook. I was angry and frightened that my family might come to know about this poem. My parents were elderly and I feared they might be very upset. My sister was extremely vulnerable.

I could perhaps have consoled myself by remembering that not all that many people read poetry.

Then again, this was electrifying. I read the poem again. I pored over the words like a medieval maiden scanning a love token. What did he mean by 'preened and patted'? That didn't sound like Richard, and what kind of subversion were they plotting? And where was the caff? I looked up 'hoplite' and found it meant an armed foot soldier in Ancient Greece.

And it was exhilarating. Thorpe had given Richard words – 'we've to change our lives for once and for all.' My brother was speaking! I realized – I do get poetry – that this might not be true. 'Poetry lies,' said Robert Lowell, a poet. It didn't matter. It was still new information, the first I'd had for thirty years. And there was my brother's voice. It didn't even matter if it wasn't his voice, if he had never said those things. It was a live connection. It could be an entire fabrication and I would still buy it.

A few marks on a page had created the illusion of life, had summoned the ghost from the neural pathways and given it a body. Words, marks, ink had made my heart race. It might not be true. It didn't matter. It didn't matter. It felt – I felt, I feel – as if that line attributed to Richard, was him speaking. And suddenly I could sympathize with those people who visit mediums, desperate to hear their loved ones speak. Here was my brother's *voice*. The bereaved relative clutches at the medium's arm. *Say more.* Thorpe had put me in touch with my brother and I was furious, exhilarated, frightened and grateful all at once. I didn't know what to do with myself. This was the first new information I had had about Richard for more than thirty years. The words, true or not, were electrifying. My inner Antigone stirred.

I wrote a letter to Thorpe at his publisher's, an incoherent mix of hurt and rage, gratitude, joy and fury all jumbled together – I was trying to work out what I thought as I went along by writing it down. What I really wanted was to know more about my brother, and Thorpe, amid apologies, promised he would tell me. In an exchange of emails he filled out a picture of a vivacious schoolmate, a true friend but one whose behaviour could be inconsiderate and reckless. Richard had behaved badly at a party while staying with the Thorpes and stolen a car; the police had been called and he had been arrested. He had run away from school to France and been tracked by Interpol. Thorpe had loved him, though, and that was what mattered. To know of more people who loved Richard could only be a good thing.

The silence had been broken and now it seemed, thanks to some change in the ether, that I was open to other signs. Through friends I met a man who was vivacious, charming, irresponsible and, on occasion, suicidal. This man told me that he had bipolar disorder. In moments of mania his behaviour could veer from careless to dangerous.

He formed embarrassing infatuations. He had stolen a car and spent the night in prison. To some extent, he said, the manic episodes could be controlled with lithium. He reminded me of Richard.

And now that word 'lithium' shone at the front of my mind. I realized that I had heard it before, in relation to Richard, although I didn't know when. Perhaps on one of those occasions that, as a child, I drifted unnoticed into a room where his behaviour was being discussed.

Adam Thorpe's correspondence made me want to seek out more connections, while I still could, but the impropriety – as it seemed to me – of contacting Richard's old friends held me back. We were living at a time when it was easy to trace old friends and contacts, restoring pathways that would, until recently, have become lost or impassable. There were countless stories of friends reunited, of marriages foundering after old relationships were rekindled. I dithered about whether to approach any of Richard's old friends. While I was dithering, one of them contacted me.

I may have got things completely wrong. But I am trying to trace an old connection. As I get older, I am more and more keen to try to discover connections.

The email was from a solicitor called Crispin, who explained that he had seen an article by me and wondered if I might be the girl he had met while staying with his friend

154

Richard one summer. He had bought my first novel, set on a farm, and deduced, through allusions to local places, that it was the same farm he had visited. Then he had traced me through Companies House where I was listed as secretary of a small charity.

The possible connection, which I have based on the above (as solicitors like to say) arises from the fact that I was lucky enough to be a friend at school and university with a wonderfully clever, generous talented and amusing boy/man – with troubles the depth of which through naivety I failed to recognize – called Richard France.

Eagerly I wrote to Crispin and received a second letter in which he told me more of what he remembered of Richard, that he was popular with girls, eloquent in debates, liked by all and a celebrity after his escapade to France. 'He wore a brown pinstripe suit on Sunday for chapel – sounds dodgy, but this was the early seventies, and it seemed cool to me.'

Crispin's most vivid memory, he said, was

going round to his rooms in New College, and seeing his hand horribly injured, and Richard telling me that he had held his hand against an electric bar fire to see what happened. I was shocked; I did not see what now seems obvious, that this showed deep troubles.

He ended the letter by saying, 'Richard is one of the people in my life I think of as admirable and wholly honourable.'

I fell on these memories, from Adam, from Crispin. All my life had been marked and shaped by the actions of someone I hadn't known very well, and about whom I could remember so little. At the heart of Antigone is a question about who owns the dead. I had thought that my family owned Richard's memory. It was liberating to see that other people could own him too.

If only I could remember more, though. There were people, family members, who could have told me about him but I still felt I couldn't ask them. Then a conversation at a Christmas party revealed an extraordinary connection. A friend of mine also knew a great friend of Richard's. For years he had known us both, but this coincidence had never come to light. All it took was for our conversation to follow one route instead of another. If it had gone another way, if I hadn't gone to the party, if I had spoken to someone different, if H had not been there, the connection might never have been revealed. But there it was and now there was a possibility of getting back in touch with RM, my brother's best friend, the last person to see him on the day he died. I found him online. I wondered what to do.

We know that memory favours significant days – the ones on which people die or are born, on which world events take place – and lets everything humdrum go. The day that my brother died in 1982 is such a marker for me that I calculate other dates around it: so, something that happened in 1977 is five years before 1982; something that happened in 1994 is 12 years after 1982. But memory has a poor grip on more mundane events. We tend to remember the fact that an event took place, the 'signpost', rather than the detail of it. As psychoanalyst Ernest Schachtel explains in 'On Memory and Childhood Amnesia', even those signposts may not designate the really important moments in a person's life, 'rather they point to the events that are conventionally supposed to be significant, to the clichés which society has come to consider as the main stations of life'.

What if we could recapture the insignificant moments too, a family supper on an ordinary Tuesday in 1980, an uneventful day at the office in 1996? What if you could return in your memory to the beach you visited thirty years ago, stoop again to pick up a shining stone that caught your eye? In the 1960s, while researching epilepsy, neurosurgeon Wilder Penfield made a remarkable discovery: patients whose brains were stimulated with electrodes retrieved memories so lifelike that they appeared 'to be a present experience'. At first Penfield thought these experiences must be dreams, but witnesses were able to verify that they were indeed the recollections of long forgotten events, prompted by Penfield's electric probe. As a result of his experiments, Penfield came to believe that all experience was perfectly preserved in memory, like a 'library of many volumes' and that it could be recovered. His research led him to conclude that 'the memory record continues intact even after the subject's ability to recall it disappears.'

The discovery seemed to hold out an astonishing promise. Our past experiences were all there, in our minds, waiting to be recovered. In theory we could learn how to drop in on some random moment in the past and relive the event contained within it. We could retrieve a memory on demand, like a computer file or a library book. It was just a question of identifying the mechanism to do that. Penfield's 'library' inevitably recalls Borges's 'Library of Babel', often referenced as a kind of bookish paradise, because it holds every book in the universe:

> When it was announced that the Library contained all books, the first reaction was unbounded joy. All men felt themselves the possessors of an intact and secret treasure. There was no personal problem, no world problem, whose eloquent solution did not exist – somewhere in some hexagon. The universe was justified; the universe suddenly became congruent with the unlimited width and breadth of humankind's hope.

If our brains were similarly capacious then perhaps we could learn how to navigate the corridors, looking for precisely the memory we wanted. Nothing need ever be forgotten. We might just need the right trigger, something like Proust's madeleine, only more dependable. Unfortunately for this theory, Borges's library turns out to be a place of torment because it's so hard to locate the right book. The answers to all life's problems are in the Library of Babel, but the chances of finding them are vanishingly small.

Borges was fascinated by these visions of infinity. Funes, a character in another of his stories, is similarly afflicted by a surfeit of information. After falling off his horse and sustaining a head injury, Funes acquires the ability to remember everything, earning him the nickname 'el Memorioso' in his Uruguayan village. Funes remembers every single thing he experiences, not only every variation of cloud shape on a particular day, but all the different sensations that every single cloud evoked. 'Two or three times he had reconstructed a whole day.' He has no choice about what he remembers because he is incapable of forgetting.

Funes's life ought to be richer because none of it is lost – every experience is stored and can be retrieved. But he has no capacity for abstract thought, so his memories aren't useful to him. 'I, myself, alone, have more memories than all mankind since the world began,' he tells the narrator. 'My memory, sir, is like a garbage heap.' Funes's condition causes him insomnia, ravages his health and contributes to his death at 19. Borges said it was reading James Joyce's *Ulysses* that gave him the idea of a man who remembers everything that happens, and 'in the end dies swept away by his infinite memory.'

What a shame Funes never met a neuroscientist, although several, including Oliver Sacks, have written about his case. Penfield's 'memory as library' theory was superseded in time, not least because the retrieval process he seemed to have discovered was identified in only a small number of patients, whose memories could not be independently verified. Subsequent research, by cognitive psychologist Elizabeth Loftus among others, has found that memories are malleable, and 'the alteration of recollection appears to be a fact of life'. We seem to remember, not an event itself, but the last time we remembered it. Memories are mere copies of other memories. A tiny number of people – perhaps sixty in the world – have hyperthemesia, giving them extraordinary powers of recall. The rest of us are programmed to forget.

Recently I reopened my teenage diaries for the first time since I wrote them decades ago and was shocked by what I found. There was page upon page about getting drunk and being sick, about fancying boys and wondering which boys fancied me, about the boys my friends fancied and whether or not these boys fancied my friends, about whether my friends liked me and whether I liked them, or preferred their boyfriends. There was a lot about going shopping – mostly for records and lip gloss – and some unoriginal outbursts: 'I don't belong in this family, whether they like it or not it's my parent's [sic] fault that I was born.'

All that was merely embarrassing. The shocking part was that on several occasions in the six months before he died, I had written that my brother was depressed, that we had had 'deep' conversations into the early hours and that I was aware of being too young and inexperienced to help him. Then, two days after his death, still aged 15 but suddenly a hundred years older, I described sitting weeping in the kitchen with my father.

D told me that Richard had definitely jumped, he had crawled out of the window of a twelfth floor and jumped off, so it wasn't an accident. I didn't want to believe it and I said 'we need never know that, he could have fallen', but D said 'No, we've got to face up to reality.'

I had tended, when remembering those days, to cast myself as the clear-eyed heroine, the one who despised euphemisms and would not turn away from the truth, however painful. My story, it turned out, was flawed. 'My truth' wasn't all that truthful after all.

It's hard to get a true picture of such long-ago events, to remember what it was like to be that child. In the years since I wrote those diary entries I had completely forgotten about the 'deep' conversations with Richard, about my awareness of his illness, my reluctance to face reality and my father's insistence on it. If I hadn't written about them, I would now never know that those conversations ever took place. Diaries may be unreliable, but they put the stories we tell ourselves in context. Perhaps they are more dependable than memories.

Our memories fail us – or do they save us in the end? Funes dies because he can't forget anything. Everything is stored, however useless, and the weight of information is paralysing. We can't move forward if memory keeps us a prisoner. So we let memories fade and then spend years, decades, lifetimes, recreating them without realizing it. We want the past to make sense, so we turn it into a story.

DAY FOUR HANDOUT:

To Brussels on Eurostar, a connection to Bruges and a 'romantic' weekend for two at a hotel called Die Swaene, one of the Small Luxury Hotels of the World, home of artful drapery, napery, fluttering waiters, candlelit everything, fine wines, fussy gastronomy and, naturally, olde worlde charme.

For my husband and myself this was something of a double-edged sword. In the period between being offered the trip and boarding the train – about a week – he had made it clear that to me that, for him at least, our marriage was not working, that he wanted to, was in fact going to, leave. Which meant, in a way, that we were already travelling; his quiet stoicism and determination and my predictable tears and anger, recriminations and shock tactics had already laid the tracks, precipitating our own, separate journeys away from each other. We decided to go to Bruges to carry on the negotiations – me trying to persuade him to stay, him building his resolve to go – on neutral territory, because at home even the half-empty packets of pasta, loo rolls and old magazines seemed to throb with a hitherto unnoticed and powerful significance: they said *All this will no longer be as it was*.

'By Waterloo Station I Sat Down and Wept'
KATHRYN FLETT, *Observer*

Day Four

Writing School

S ome people want to be writers more than they want
to write. They're mesmerized by the mythology, the
paraphernalia. Reverently they contemplate the little table
where Jane Austen wrote her novels, peer in at the writing
hut, lost in Welsh woods, where Dylan Thomas wrote *Under
Milk Wood*. Roald Dahl peered into Thomas's writing shed
once and liked it so much that he went off to build one for
himself – and now people can peer into that one, too.

I've looked through my fair share of windows – in
at Virginia Woolf's writing studio at Monk's House
in Sussex, or out at the Pacific as I stood beside Pablo
Neruda's desk on the Chilean coast, trying to see what the
poet would have seen when he wrote his epic poem *Canto
General*. I have peered through the window that inspired

Emily Brontë when she wrote *Wuthering Heights*. Can we see what they saw? Can we get some of what they had? A tea towel only takes you so far.

We watch films about writers, read books about writers, carry tote bags with the faces and thoughts of writers. *Thinking is my fighting.* We tweet about writers. We sit in audiences where someone is always going to ask 'Where do you get your ideas from?' and someone else will always want to know if there's a particular pen or book or ritual on which the writer depends. And another person will always make an observation that isn't a question as such ... we're looking for the key to creativity. We're obsessed with writers' problems, their drinking habits, their mental health. Their failings only make them more attractive and we envy the people who sleep with writers, even though they regularly tell us – sometimes in poems and novels of their own – what a grievous mistake that was. In 2010 David Foster Wallace lamented that he hadn't yet got laid on the *Infinite Jest* book tour. But in 1977 John Cheever got sucked off 'in almost every room' at the Yaddo writer's colony, and 'tried unsuccessfully to mount a young man on the bridge between the lakes'. In 1941, also at Yaddo, Carson McCullers prostrated herself outside the door of Katherine Anne Porter. The object of her infatuation simply stepped over her, without saying a word.

It was Friday, our last day at the writing school, and the atmosphere was charged, as it inevitably will be in a house where twelve strangers have spent four days together and talked about worries and secrets they may never have shared with anyone else.

'How is everyone?' Tom asked tenderly as we all took our places around the table. He was good at the nurturing aspect of this work. Another time when we had taught together, a participant became overwhelmed while trying to read a piece about her father at the end-of-week performance. Tom had swept her into his arms, led her to a seat, then asked permission to read her piece aloud himself, which of course he did beautifully, while she watched sniffing.

'How have you found the week? Did it meet expectations? Have you got what you were hoping for?'

'What I hope is that you're going to talk about getting an agent today,' said Peter. 'It was my main reason for coming.'

'We'll definitely get to that,' I said stiffly, remembering how Peter had tried to blackmail me at the start of the week.

'Can I just say,' said Jules, waving the morning's handout, 'how much I hated this?'

It was a piece by Kathryn Flett, a classic, I thought, of travel writing, because in between accepting the commission for a cushy freebie – a romantic weekend break in Bruges for two – and making the trip, Flett's husband announced that he was leaving her. They decided to go together on the weekend anyway, and Flett produced a travel piece that dutifully ticked all the boxes required of a journalist on a press junket, while cleverly subverting the genre by weaving in the devastation she felt about the unexpected end to her marriage.

We arrived at 9 p.m., just in time for dinner, and were given the best table at the back of the restaurant, which has been converted into a conservatory. Our package – oh irony! – was called the 'Romeo and Juliet weekend' and included two set meals, one of four courses, one of six, with wine and, according to the brochure, the threat of champagne being opened by a sword, which is the kind of thing I hate. I wondered if we could borrow the sword afterwards. We didn't have champagne.

'Why did you hate it, Jules?,' said Tom. 'Talk me through this.'

'Just, the relentless bloody negative tone.'

'I thought it was funny!' said Jim in a rare divergence of opinion from Jules.

'She did have quite a lot to feel negative about,' said Susie. 'Her marriage was ending.'

'She exposes him,' said Sheena. 'He didn't ask to be in the piece.'

'He could have refused to go,' reasoned Jim. 'And we don't know that she didn't show him the piece first. Maybe she was the one paying the mortgage.'

'Plus he got a freebie out of it', said Sam.

'Even so,' said Zoe.

'She hardly exposes him at all,' said Diana. 'It's all about her. It's the most gratingly solipsistic piece I've ever read.'

'Did nobody like it then?' said Tom.

'I liked it,' said Lily, blushing violently. Every observation she made induced a physical reaction in which all of us seemed to share some part. 'It sounded as though she was writing from the heart, but it was clever too.'

'Is it ever OK,' I asked, 'to write about other people without their permission?'

'Not unless they're dead!' said Diana. During the course of the week I had noticed that she often mentioned death with a kind of relish.

'It's quite impossible to write about people without exploiting them,' said Peter. 'If you're expecting to make money out of your book then it is literal exploitation, unless you enter into a financial arrangement with the people portrayed.'

'You can change people's names, I guess,' ventured Kisi.

'I don't think you should worry about what other people think. It's important to speak your truth,' said Zoe. 'Wouldn't you say?'

I nodded briefly. Actually I hated the idea of 'your truth' and 'my truth'. Of course everybody has a different version of an event, but someone who insists on the primacy of 'my truth' seems to be announcing their unwillingness to hear anyone else's. In real life, 'my story' intersects with other people's; 'my truth' may not be universally acknowledged. We used to talk of telling 'my side of the story.' Now we seemed determined to stake a claim to the whole story, all of the truth.

Writer Blake Morrison once quipped that there's no word so narcissistic as 'memoir': it has 'me' and 'moi' in it. Yet Morrison has produced two works of memoir, about his mother and father, and seemed not narcissistic at all when he came to speak on a course I taught once, but generous and friendly. He advised his students to write their book first and only then consider the potential hurt to people who appeared in it. 'You can't write as though your aunt were looking over your shoulder.'

But when one person writes about another, they create a power imbalance in *real* life – the one that happens outside books and sometimes seems less compelling to writers. Unless the other person is also writer with a publishing deal their only option may be to keep a dignified silence, or take their chances on social media. Rachel Cusk has written about the failure of her first marriage – mostly holding herself accountable – but we have never heard from her husband. Sheila Heti's novel *How Should A Person Be?*, is based on emails and taped conversations with people she knows, especially her close friend Margaux. Heti describes it as a work of 'constructed reality', as real and as fake as reality TV. Margaux read forty drafts of it, and presumably approved the final one.

What of those people who don't get a veto, who don't approve? Perhaps that's an injustice we should put up with for the sake of literature, especially when it leads to works of art such as Graham Greene's *The End of the Affair* or Harold Pinter's *Betrayal*. Sometimes, though, I liked to imagine that down the road, in the half light of the misty valley, there was another residential centre where all the people whose lives had provided material for writers got to tell their own side of the story. The fathers and mothers written off as cruel or neglectful, the bad lovers, the tragically dead, all stepped out of the narrative and offered up an alternative version of events.

By Grand Central Station I sat down and wept – to which Flett's title playfully alludes – is Elizabeth Smart's classic account of falling in love with the poet George Barker, first published in 1945 and still enticing readers with the wild romance of its title and premise. Smart claimed to have fallen in love with George Barker on reading a volume of his poetry, and it's an arresting image: a woman picks up some poems in a second-hand bookshop and, right there in the shop, falls so deeply in love with the author that soon she is raising funds for him *and his wife* to join her at the Writers' Colony in Big Sur, California. How good must a collection of poetry be to induce someone to change their life, right there on the spot? The turbulent love affair that ensued produced four children, several memoirs and a lot of grief.

And here's another transatlantic literary affair, with links to another writers' colony, this time Yaddo. That was where, in 1948, American writers Robert Lowell and Elizabeth Hardwick embarked on a relationship that was

to last more than twenty years and seemed happy enough –
tested though it was by Lowell's bipolar depression and
frequent visits to hospital – until he failed to return from
a teaching stint in England: he had begun an affair with
Lady Caroline Blackwood, literary socialite and ex-wife of
Lucien Freud.

As the months went by Hardwick wrote her husband
long letters, reminding him that wife and daughter needed
him back. Lowell had left everything hanging she said,
itemising his belongings like William Trevor itemizes
Leary's. 'Your things, you, your life, your family, your
clothes, your work, your old shoes, ties, winter coats, books,
everything seems sitting about at every turn.'

She felt sure Lowell's infatuation wouldn't last. And
she kept writing to him, furiously and lovingly and always
worried about money, tax and their daughter Harriet's
schooling.

Lowell saw the potential of these angry, lyrical letters as
material for a new long poem he was writing. He had used
his family in poems before; he was, after all, America's
first and most famous 'confessional poet'. Now, improbably
secluded in the Sussex countryside, he started working on
The Dolphin, a long poem about the end of his marriage,
his new relationship with Blackwood, and the birth of their
son. Hardwick's letters had been written in anguish; they
were private. But Lowell had felt the shiver: they were too
good not to use. 'The letters make the book', he explained
to a friend. 'I couldn't bear to have my book (my life) wait

inside me like a dead child.' Of all the methods used by writers to justify betrayal, comparing your work to a child who may die must be the worst.

The poet Elizabeth Bishop, an old friend of Lowell's, thought the use of the letters unconscionable. Lowell had changed the order of events, attributed to Hardwick lines she didn't quite say. It was 'infinite mischief', she said, to mix up fact and fiction this way. 'One can use one's life as material – one does, anyway – but these letters – aren't you violating a trust? . . . Art just isn't worth that much.'

It is hard to escape the idea that, even as he was writing to his wife and child, Lowell was thinking of lines that might look good in a poem. And he was picking over her letters, including ones where she expressed her reservations about this, cherry picking phrases and images, changing the syntax here and there, editing and 'improving' her. He alters her words to fit the rhythm and timbre he needs, and changes the meaning along with it. 'The original is heart-breaking but interminable', he tells Bishop, as though he has done Hardwick a favour by editing her words. But it is also strange that Hardwick keeps on writing lyrical letters, as though daring Lowell to use them, waiting to see how she will be traduced.

Art just isn't worth that much. Bishop's protestation has become famous, but so has the advice Hardwick gave Lowell much earlier in their relationship, when he was testing the limits of confessional writing. 'Why not say what happened?' she told him – as if such a thing were straightforward. For no one can ever say exactly what happened. Once the moment has passed, there is no single way to represent it truthfully.

Recently writers have been falling out of love with fiction. Rachel Cusk says she has come to 'mistrust stories', that it's embarrassing 'making up John and Jane and having them do things together.' Similarly, Sheila Heti finds fictional characters boring. 'It seems so tiresome to make up a fake person and put them through the paces of a fake story.'

But it's disingenuous to see non-fiction as any more truthful. It isn't possible to write about real people without moving them into the literary realm. This was what Hardwick feared – that she and her daughter had become characters in someone else's work. Once you decide to use real events, real people in an essay or memoir, contrivance is unavoidable; you 'storify' people who are real. You allow real events, like the death of someone, to be useful to you, to provide structure and meaning in your own story. It feels dishonourable.

Then again life needs to be written about – and rendered in paint, music, film and theatre. Our stories won't fit neatly on a page, so there's no choice but to shape them. It isn't possible to say exactly 'what happened' – but we can still try.

There were various inflammatory post-it notes around the kitchen now. 'This kills trees' on the kitchen towel and 'meat is murder' on the fridge. Lynn had gone, so who was putting them up? I suspected Zoe. Last night a row had spilled out of the kitchen into the main room when she accused Peter of creating a 'patriarchal atmosphere'.

'What patriarchal thing did he do?' I asked.

'He said he shouldn't have to wash up, that it was women's work.'

'He was winding you up, Zoe. He doesn't really think that.' I tried not to sound exasperated, but since there were twice as many women in the house as men, Peter's patriarchy ought to be easily contained.

'What's the point, though,' Zoe said, and then Kisi had appeared indignantly behind her, ready with a witness statement if one were needed and holding a tea towel as evidence.

'I know. It's tiring.' I shrugged. 'What can you do.'

'He's a twat,' said Zoe.

'He's a total arse,' added Kisi.

'Look, why don't you two go out for a walk? It's a beautiful evening. I'll handle Peter.'

I was weary of nurturing people all day, tending not only to their creativity, but all their other needs – it felt like a duty never fully dispatched, one symbolized by the high-vis jacket that hung shimmering on my bedroom door all night.

They had been four intense days, twelve of us folded into this house in the hills and then into even smaller spaces within it, the snug, the meeting room, the steam-filled kitchen. I had spent hours in the shed listening to stories, with the merest glimpse of the world outside it. Cups of tea,

174

the British way of showing love, were endlessly thrust into my hands. I tramped back and forth from the downstairs loo with its old chain flush. I read thousands of words and even at night, in bed, I was working through structures and scenarios, thinking of ways to turn my students' stories into books.

Today Zoe seemed in a better mood. She and Kisi had picked elderflower heads while out on their walk the previous evening and were steeping them to make a cocktail for our last night. Sam was going off to buy some vodka and at lunch there was some discussion about suitable names for the cocktail. 'Writers' Ruin,' Diana suggested.

'Ah come on,' Jim said with a wink. 'Not all writers are drunks.'

'The best ones are,' Diana said. 'Think of Dorothy Parker, Scott Fitzgerald, Hemingway' – it was clear that Diana planned to enumerate a lot of brilliant drunks and that nobody was going to pay much attention.

'Tell you what, though, I'll miss this food,' said Sam, through a mouthful of microwaved leftovers.

'Keep shovelling it in,' said the centre director as he passed through the kitchen. 'There's no course next week and we want everything finished up.'

'What made you want to be a writer, if you don't mind me asking?' said Sheena, who was sitting next to me at the table.

'Hard to say. I loved reading when I was growing up,' I said. 'I probably glamourized it.'

175

I used to pore over black and white photographs of Iris Murdoch and Muriel Spark in cardigans, frowning at their typewriters through clouds of smoke. I still buy cardigans with these role models in mind and miss my old typewriter. It was only when I was writing my first book that the words began to seem more compelling than the accessories. It was so exhilarating to speak freely, and to think that you could hold someone's attention, make them laugh, even, just with marks on a page. A friend told me she had seen someone bump into a lamppost while reading my book and I was delighted to be the subject of a comedy trope. I never feel more myself than when I'm writing.

Yet it's embarrassing to call yourself 'a writer'. The word sounds hubristic, looks silly on a passport and seems to be tempting fate because, even if this year and last year went well, next year may be a disaster. Sometimes you tell people you're a writer and you can see them prickle with irritation, as if wanting to shake you out of a delusion. But if you don't delude yourself that you can be a writer, how will you ever find the motivation to try?

'What about you, Sheena? Why do you want to write?' I asked. 'What spurs you on?'

'I want my book in Tesco, by the till,' she said, with a defiant smile. 'I want everyone I know to see it there. All those people who tried to write me off.'

Across the table Kisi raised her hand for a high five but had to drop it when, in one of those surprising lurches of mood, Sheena's face crumpled and her defiance gave way to tears.

'Hey babe, your book *is* going to be in Tesco!' said Kisi, squeezing Sheena's arm instead. 'We're all going to buy it there!'

Everyone agreed we would and Sheena nodded tearfully. I asked her whether she would like a cup of tea or coffee.

'Tea,' Sheena gasped.

In the kitchen, waiting for the kettle to boil, I overheard Susie telling Jules:

'I feel as if your romantic life is taking off just as mine is ending.'

'You'll get another shot, I bet,' Jules said. 'You're too beautiful not to. Tell you what,' she put her plate down on the counter. 'Let's dress up tonight. It's our last night together. Let's all swap something.' She looked at me. 'What have you got to swap?'

'Um, my diamanté hair slide?'

'Very swish,' said Jules. Her eyes widened. 'And we can get the girls to give us festival make-up!'

After lunch Tom and I posed for the photographer who came to take pictures for the centre's collection and then I returned to the shed, for the last private session of the week. Diana sat down opposite me and folded her arms in a defensive attitude, as though challenging me to force the story out of her. She wasn't going let it go without thumb-screws or waterboarding.

'I should have brought you some tea. I'm sorry I didn't

think of it,' Diana said, so matter-of-factly that it was clear she had never intended to bring tea and didn't feel sorry that she hadn't.

'Honestly, I'm glad you didn't.'

'I found this morning's session very interesting. Instructive.'

'That's good. Because of the letters you're thinking of publishing?'

Her arms unfolded then and she leaned forward, positioning a cupped right hand on the table in front of her and moving imaginary quantities from one area to another as she spoke, like one of those con artists you see on Oxford Street, with three cups and a ball.

'The letters are from my mother, in fact. But I never knew she was my mother, you see. I always thought she was my *sister*.' Ta-da: no ball. A little waggle of the head, almost comic, almost music hall.

'Jesus.'

'Well indeed, but you know it wasn't uncommon. Teenage pregnancies were often covered up that way, especially in large working-class families.'

'Isn't there someone famous . . . ?'

'Bound to be a few of them,' said Diana, touching her tongue to a back tooth.

Then she told me how, aged just fifteen, her mother had got pregnant by a boy at school and been sent away to an aunt to have the baby. Diana had been brought up by her grandmother as another sibling. Her mother was the eldest of four, so it was easy to pass the new baby off as a fifth sibling, especially since the family had often moved because her father was regularly out of work.

'There weren't a lot of people around who would have known,' Diana said.

'What was she like, when you were growing up? Did she seem motherly to you?'

Diana folded her arms more tightly, mimicking a mother's embrace. 'In a sense she was, I suppose, but then she was the eldest, so you might say the role fell to her.'

'And when did you find out?'

'Not until after she had died. She got cancer in her early forties. And that was when my brother and sisters told me. Or rather, my aunt and uncle, as I then found out they were, told me. They had promised her they would keep the secret.'

'So they all knew and you didn't?'

Diana nodded slowly and I thought I saw her eyes glisten. 'My grandparents had told them. I was the only person in the family who didn't know. That was almost the worst of it, oddly, feeling that everyone else was in on a secret I knew nothing about. It makes you feel stupid.'

'I bet. Were you angry?'

She began moving the imaginary pieces again.

'I don't know how much it helps to be angry. I had a good upbringing, after all. I know people who were mistreated as children, neglected. I had a happy, secure childhood, so I can't complain.'

'But one based on a lie.'

'A lie was woven into it. Yes.' She looked sharply at me. 'Do you think lies are always harmful?'

'My hunch is that they are.' I had written about the children of Argentina's 'disappeared' who were brought up in military families and never learned about their real parents until traced by a humanitarian group, The Grandmothers of May Square. Even the children who had no inkling of the truth seemed to have been affected physically, as well as psychologically,

'But who knows? All of us are surrounded by lies to one degree or another,' I said, 'especially when we're children and we don't know the full picture. So I guess it's more complicated than balancing love against harm. Where do the letters come in?'

'She wrote them to me every so often, almost like a kind of diary, without ever sending them. They were about her feelings, how proud she was, that kind of thing. When I got into Oxford, you know, and then the Foreign Office. She kept all the letters together in a box, so I suppose she did want me to know the truth one day, eventually.' She shivered, brusquely. 'Don't you find it very cold here? It must be about ten degrees colder than it is outside.'

'I come prepared' – I showed her the hot water bottle under my jumper – 'but, your mother – she must have been bursting with pride, and she couldn't tell you. The letters were her only outlet.'

Diana nodded again, carefully, not speaking.

'Or do you feel she could have told you, should have done?'

'I don't know why she didn't. She must have thought I had a loving relationship with the woman I thought was my mother – my grandmother, in other words – and she didn't want to damage it. She may have tried to show me she was proud in other ways. I can't remember.'

'What's the plan with the letters, then?'

'Well, I've given that a lot of thought. And I've decided now: I'm going to put them back in their box and keep them in a drawer.'

'You're not going to –'

'No, I've decided that I don't want to publish them, after all.'

'Why, though? Did I say something in the session this morning that put you off?'

'Not at all. I've just realized that my strengths lie in other areas. I'm not someone who's good at investigating feelings. I'm probably too pragmatic for that. I haven't got the patience, to be honest. There are other writing projects I can pursue. Probably nothing publishable; but getting published isn't everything, is it?'

'Definitely not. I hope you don't feel this week's been a waste of time.'

'Far from it! Deciding not to write a book is as useful as deciding you are going to write one. I think I'll just enjoy writing for its own sake.'

'That's admirable – if only more of us could feel like that.' And as Diana stood up I said, 'I hope you don't mind me asking, but did you ever work in Intelligence? Apparently Peter thinks you did.'

Her laughter bounced off the walls. 'You know what Peter's like – he loves a good story.' And she was still laughing as she walked away back up to the house.

'There's a man at my gym who has "I AM ENOUGH" tattooed on his arm,' I said to Tom, as we sat together outside the kitchen for the last time, drinking wine. Our bottles were on the ground in front of us, each labelled with our initials. Everybody would be packing up and leaving the next morning, and already there was a sense of sad departure in the air. 'Big letters, right across his forearm,' I said. 'You have to wonder – why? I mean, I—'

'You've gone out,' said Tom, passing me the lighter.

'Thanks. I get the reason. He's been through some terrible event. Perhaps his confidence was crushed. He's still dealing with trauma and this helps. But why does he need to involve everyone else in his psychodrama? People must always be asking him why it's there, and then he has to keep on explaining, going over events ...'

Tom tapped his roll-up and the stub of ash fell neatly into a flower pot. 'Perhaps he wants people to ask. He doesn't want to live with a secret.'

'I never would ask though – would you?'

'No, but I was brought up to keep my feelings private, probably you were too.'

'I had a teacher who told me not to expose myself,' I said,

and it sounded so absurd, said aloud, that we both laughed. 'It means that I know this really personal thing about the man at the gym even though we've never spoken. He's got no chance of presenting himself as a blank canvas. Isn't it important, the blank canvas?'

'He could just wear long sleeves.'

'Right, at the gym?'

Tom looked over his shoulder towards the kitchen window. We could hear the sound of pans being crashed about, of laughter and raised voices.

'Oh my God, Sam!' we heard Zoe shriek. 'If you do that again you're literally dead!' More crashing was followed by a chorus of cheers.

'Do you think it's safe to go inside? I'm starving,' Tom said.

'Come on then. Let's go and see what's going on.'

We all cleared up together after the last evening meal, everyone wrangling in the kitchen over washing and drying methods. Jim thought it was fine to leave the plates sudsy as they drained; Diana insisted the suds be rinsed away; Zoe said it was wasteful to leave the tap running. Then we set off in groups down the road to a small building designated the 'theatre', where the participants were going to perform their finished pieces. Sam and Nick had gathered these together into stapled anthologies for everyone. During the course of the week there seemed to have been a collective recognition among the group of Nick's oddness, and a willingness to accommodate it.

A festival atmosphere accompanied our procession, with Zoe and Kisi at the head of the parade, carrying a large bowl of elderflower and vodka. Out of the corner of my eye I saw Peter, looming up on my left. 'I thought you'd like to know that I gave you a seven,' he said.

'Sorry, I'm not with you, Peter.'

'On the feedback form. A seven.'

'You mean bastard!' said Jim jovially, from the other side of me. His arm was wrapped around Jules, who was walking between us.

'A seven is perfectly reasonable!' Peter expostulated. 'Generous, even!' I realized now that he liked goading people into a reaction so that he could enjoy these brisk, defensive outbursts, and decided not to play the game.

'A seven's fair', I agreed, 'but don't tell me anything else about what you put on the feedback form. That's between you and your god, Peter.'

'I gave you a ten, darling,' murmured Jules, putting her arm through mine and pulling me closer, so that I was almost within Jim's embrace too. We strode together down the path like three friends off to see the wizard.

In the theatre the performance was soon underway, every reading greeted with applause and cheers. We listened in respectful silence to Sheena's account of almost being murdered by her neighbour, and whooped at the end, when she asserted that this ordeal had only made her stronger; she would never be frightened again.

Tom rushed to the stage to help Sheena dismount it, then

stayed to thank everyone for a week in which, he said, we had both learned as much as they all had. My diamanté hair slide sparkled in his hair. I was wearing a necklace borrowed from Jules, who wore Diana's scarf. Peter and Nick had traded watches. Lily had on some piece of festival froufrou borrowed from Zoe who had earlier doled out stars and sparkles from her makeup pouch. Everyone raised their glasses and clapped. I felt a tension in my throat, an urge to cry, and pushed against it. I turned to Nick, who was sitting behind me.

'I really hope you've enjoyed this, that you've had a good week,' I said to him.

'It's been one of the best weeks of my life,' Nick said, without irony, three gold stars glittering on one of his cheeks.

We headed back towards the house, then, swinging our empty glasses. Sam realized he had forgotten his anthology and trotted back to get it. A clear moon, almost full, hung above the woods where I had been lost earlier in the week, and some people decided to branch off and walk across the fields to the village, hoping to reach the pub before last orders. They waited for Sam to catch up, then off they went, along the dirt track, lights from their phones dancing ahead of them as they walked. We could hear Kisi and Zoe laughing as they got further away.

'Oh to be young,' said Jules.

'You're hardly old,' I said. 'Come on, let's get drunk.'

The rest of us walked back to the house and stayed up late talking about our lives, our plans and the things we wanted to write about. We were still talking by the time the others came back from the pub, and through the window we saw Sam perform a perfect cartwheel across the grass.

Endings

I recognized him as soon as the train came into the station. People don't really change much, not even over the course of thirty-five years, which was the time that had elapsed since I last saw my brother's best friend.

We hugged each other and walked to his car. Soon we were driving up into the South Downs, into that landscape made so familiar by Eric Ravilious that to visit it almost feels like a magic trick, like entering a picture book. We parked and began to walk towards Firle Beacon. We talked about our families and work, the shape our lives had taken over three decades. My parents had both died in the last few years. RM had spent time travelling in Africa, left a punishing job for something more fulfilling. The conversation moved towards Richard with no awkward silences or changes in gear. He had been the best company, said RM, a loyal friend, a soul mate. They had shared many dark moments, but also times of great happiness.

I looked down at the houses comfortingly arrayed in the valley below us. Here I was, reunited with one of my brother's friends decades after his death. It was hard to believe in this moment and I wondered how to make it real, how to keep it for posterity. To think that for years RM had been so close at hand, practically within my own circle of friends, and that we hadn't known about our shared connection.

'Recently I've been wondering if Richard could have had bipolar,' I said to RM. It was painful to say this, at last. 'Would that make sense?'

'Yes, I think so,' said RM. 'He was very up and down. He could be impetuous. Sometimes we had to bundle him out of parties before he did something awful.'

I remembered the stories of rebellion, of missed job interviews, of rows and resignations abruptly tendered. Richard once told me how he had climbed out of the window of a restaurant toilet when he realized he couldn't pay the bill. As a timid child I admired his daring. And as a teenager, I was proud to think I might have a similarly rebellious streak. 'You are like me,' he had told me, when in fact I was very different: a cautious child and a compliant adult. All my life I had wanted to make up to my parents for their sorrows. And now I had a different perspective on my brother's story, could look at it from above, almost, as I was looking down on the houses in this Sussex valley, following their connection via roads and footpaths. The recollections

I had gathered from Richards's friends added up to such a sad picture. Recently I had also been in touch with one of his teachers, who still remembered him. He had been struck, this man said, by the way my brother combined untidiness with elegance and how that seemed to point to other paradoxes. Richard liked people but didn't mind about their feelings. 'He favoured truth over falsehood more – if you see what I mean – than goodness over evil. He was intellectually curious, but strove for effect rather than an objective goal.' I wondered if this was the teacher who had written that Richard was destined for triumph or disaster. 'I think we're all going to have to accept that the enigma of his death is never going to become intelligible.'

I realized that I would never really understand the man who had been my brother because I had only ever known part of the story. I would have to content myself with fractured memories, a few books and photographs and the precious evidence of my diaries.

At the brow of the hill we found a patch of grass to sit on and take in the view. RM described how, on the night before my brother died, they had all been at the pub and Richard had seemed in good spirits, laughing and telling jokes. That was one of the reasons his death seemed to make no sense. I knew – because I had read about this phenomenon – that such behaviour isn't uncharacteristic of people who have finally taken the decision to end their lives; the agonizing is over and there may be a sense of relief, of wanting to leave loved ones with a happy last memory.

The next morning Richard had shouted from the shower for someone to chuck him a towel and RM had passed him one, though not actually seen him before he left the house.

'That disembodied hand holding the towel around the bathroom door – it still haunts me,' said RM. 'He didn't speak a word. Perhaps I should have known something was wrong.'

After that my brother apparently walked for an hour or two before reaching the building where he ended his life. I wondered if he had crossed paths on the way with anyone who could see that he was in trouble, if anyone had spoken to him. RM said he had felt guilty, because he had been going through a low period himself and they had often talked about suicide. Sometimes they jokingly quoted a line from John Irving's novel *The Hotel New Hampshire*, 'keep passing the open windows'. It's a phrase the different members of the hotelier family in the book repeat to one another. Their lives are complicated, and there are a lot of windows in the hotel.

On the day my brother walked out of his house for the last time, he left a copy of *The Hotel New Hampshire* on his bed opened to the last page, where the final line is, 'You have to keep passing the open windows.' I remembered how my father had feared that Richard might have left a suicide note. Instead he had left this. His last communication with the world had been a line from a book.

How awful it must have been for the flatmates, all in their twenties, to find that message. I thought of the words he spoke in Adam Thorpe's poem, 'we've to change our lives.' For how long, how many years had he kept trying to believe a change might be possible, before deciding that it wasn't? I mourned the life, the different lives, Richard might have lived; the father, partner, uncle he might have been. We had all missed out on so much.

'I don't think Richard realized that he was going to be dead for so long,' RM said, and we both smiled at this absurd truth. What do you know, really at twenty-five, or at fifteen, or forty-five, sixty-five, ninety-five? Life doesn't get any less mysterious. If you are ill and frightened, it must seem endlessly cruel.

'You should write about this,' RM said.

After walking we went down into the village and had lunch at a pub then sat drinking and talking in the sun. When we parted at the station it was with assurances that we would see each other again. And we have seen each other, and it no longer feels necessary to talk about Richard.

I read *The Hotel New Hampshire*, of course, and heartily disliked it. I hadn't read any Irving before and found the zany style tiresome, especially when applied to themes of rape and prostitution. Essentially the novel is a shaggy dog story about an eccentric family who run a series of hotels and own a pet bear. One of them does, in fact, kill herself by jumping through an open window. A paragraph on the last page, a ham-fisted tribute to F. Scott Fitzgerald, seemed to contain a message for me.

So we dream on. Thus we invent our lives. We give ourselves a sainted mother, we make our father a hero; and
someone's older brother, and someone's older sister – they
become our heroes, too. We invent what we love, and
what we fear. There is always a brave, lost brother – and a
little lost sister, too. We dream on and on: the best hotel,
the perfect family, the resort life. And our dreams escape
us almost as vividly as we can imagine them.

I hated to think this could have been a decisive last read
for my brother. Did Irving's strange novel put the idea of
suicide in his head, or help formulate it somehow? No, the
idea must have been there for a long time, perhaps even
for years. Would I have preferred him to leave something
different? I suppose so, but we can only shape our own lives.

My daughter calls me on FaceTime from her room at university. I used to avoid speaking to faces on a screen, but
since lockdown I've learned to get more comfortable with
these technologies, as all of us have had to. She's writing
an essay on Antigone, her first at university, comparing
Anouilh's version to Sophocles'. The title of her essay is
'The Necessary Death of Antigone'.

'I'm not looking for any advice, as such, I just want to
read it to someone.'

'Sure, go ahead,' I say and try to concentrate on the
essay as she reads it, although I'm distracted by this nov-
elty – my daughter's lovely face, in a little frame propped

up against books on my desk. I still can't help marvelling at the innovations of the digital age and I often imagine myself explaining them to Richard – 'People hardly ever use money. Everyone walks around with a coffee. We all carry mini computers that can tell you everything you need to know.' Outside a gust of wind catches the slim branches of my rowan tree, overbalancing a heavy pigeon that had been picking at the berries.

'Thoughts?' says my daughter, from her little frame.

'It's quite bleak. You think Antigone allows herself to be buried alive only because she has no reason to keep on living?'

'She's a nihilist, so yes.'

'What about her duty to her brother?'

'That's just an excuse. In Sophocles' version she's fulfilling an obligation to the gods but in this one she's an atheist, so there are no gods to appease.'

'Does it actually say she's an atheist? I can't remember now. It's years since I read it.'

'I think it's pretty obvious,' says my daughter, with an eighteen-year-old's cool assurance.

'What about doing it for love then? You don't think she loves him?'

'Well, there is a hint at something incestuous, but basically no. She's incapable of any kind of human connection. Hang on, you've frozen. Hello?'

'No, I'm just thinking. I hadn't remembered that aspect of the play, to be honest. I thought she loved him.'

193

'No, not really. Anything else?'

'Well – just a thought.'

'Go on then.'

'Can you say that there are no gods in Anouilh's version because he has substituted himself? The author is God, etc.'

'Like in that play by Pirandesi.'

'Pirandello.'

'I could talk about that. I don't know. I've only got forty-three words, though.'

'Oh, OK,' I say. 'Well I think it's great – well done! How's everything otherwise?'

'It's fine, but I've got to go now. I need to finish this and send it off.'

'Did you get the package I sent?'

'Yeah, thanks. Actually could you send some tights?'

'Of course. Interesting or plain?'

'Whatever you think. Interesting, maybe.'

'Are you managing to meet people, despite lockdown?'

'Yeah it's not too bad really. It's all fine. I'll tell you about it later, OK?'

'OK.'

'Bye then.'

'Bye.'

'Don't put on the sad face!'

'I'm not! This is just how my face is.'

'OK, well anyway, speak to you soon.'

'Promise me you're taking care of yourself.'

'Of course I am! I'm not even that homesick.'

'That's good. I'll send the tights ASAP.'
'Thanks. And I'll call you soon, OK?'
'OK, Bye, then. Maybe speak at the weekend?'
'Sounds good. Bye!'
'Bye. Look after yourself.'
'I will. Bye!'
'Bye.'
'Bye!'

Goodbye
Goodbye
Goodbye.

A Note on Sources

All writing is a negotiation between experience and imagination. Memory adds a wild card because, as Ernest Schachtel notes in 'On Memory and Childhood Amnesia', 'What is remembered is usually, more or less, only the fact that such an event took place. The signpost is remembered, not the place, the thing, the situation to which it points.' Elizabeth Loftus observed in 'Misfortunes of Memory' that 'the alteration of recollection appears to be a fact of life'. Wilder Penfield's experiments are discussed in Alison Winter's *Memory: Fragments of a Modern History*.

Yet childhood is an irresistible source, because it's such a rich period of half-understood experience, a time of mysteries and mistakes. The young Dylan Thomas couldn't understand why so many men failed to come back from the Front. Was their front hall really so dangerous? My favourite account of childhood is Laura Shaine Cunningham's wonderfully subversive *Sleeping Arrangements*.

Growing up in the country, I was lucky to have a father who knew a great deal about nature. (I remember him opening up an owl pellet to show me the tiny, complete skeleton of a field mouse inside it.) The Northern Irish poet Seamus Heaney strikes many rich allusions between his country childhood and his adult preoccupations, so it was amusing to hear his son Michael admit that he 'wasn't especially fond of the outdoors'. That quote is from the BBC documentary, *Seamus Heaney and the Music of What Happens*. Heaney's poem 'Blackberry Picking' can be found in *Opened Ground: Poems 1966–1996*. Mark Twain wrote about travelling through the Rockies in *Roughing It* in 1872. Helen Macdonald's memoir *H is for Hawk* describes her exhilarating immersion in the wild world of a goshawk. Nature writing has been flowering – so to speak – in recent years, although there are some dissenters. Kathleen Jamie's analysis of the word 'wild' comes from 'A Lone Enraptured Male' (her review of Robert Macfarlane's *The Wild Places*) published in the *London Review of Books*. Sylvia Plath's poem 'Sheep in Fog' can be found in *Ariel*.

While we're with the poets, lines on bereavement quoted from William Wordsworth are from 'Elegiac Stanzas Suggested by a Picture of Peele Castle in a Storm', which can be found on the Poetry Foundation website, an excellent resource. Robert Pack's commentary on them is in *The Long View: Essays on the Discipline of Hope and Poetic*

Craft. Robert Frost's 'The Road Not Taken' is from his 1916 collection *Mountain Interval*. Craig Raine used the phrase 'tender blister' in his poem 'Gethsemane', and it was Elizabeth Bishop who argued 'art just isn't worth that much' in a letter to Robert Lowell. She was responding to a draft of his poetry collection *The Dolphin*; their correspondence is included in *The Dolphin Letters*, edited by Saskia Hamilton. When Bishop spoke of the 'infinite mischief' of 'mixing fact and fiction in unknown proportions' she was quoting from a letter Thomas Hardy wrote to a friend. Hoping to allay his wife's fears about the poem, while it was still a draft, Lowell wrote to Hardwick, 'My story is both a composition and alas, a rather grinding autobiography ... though of course one neither does nor should tell the literal or ultimate truth. Poetry lies.'

Perhaps diaries are more truthful. I'm grateful to Faber and Faber for permission to quote from *The Journals of Sylvia Plath*, edited by Karen V. Kukil. Virginia Woolf's recommendation to 'arrange whatever pieces come your way' comes from *A Writer's Diary* (Persephone Books). Her thoughts on 'street haunting' are from an essay of the same name, originally published in the Yale Review in 1927. The 'Oxford Street Tide' is one of five essays written for *Good Housekeeping Magazine* in 1931–32 and published together as *The London Scene: Five Essays by Virginia Woolf* in 1975. Charles Dickens first wrote about his nocturnal wandering in 'Night Walks with the Uncommercial Traveller', published in his own weekly magazine *All The Year Round* in 1860.

Blake Morrison's observation that memoir can be narcissistic, (because it has both 'me' and 'moi' in it) comes from an essay in *On Life-Writing*. We readers love these personal accounts, all the same, and I am particularly grateful to Fourth Estate for freely granting permission for an extract from Lorna Sage's brilliant memoir *Bad Blood*, and to Kathryn Flett for extracts from her ingenious travel piece 'By Waterloo Station I Sat Down and Wept', which first appeared in the *Observer* in 1997. Joan Didion's treatise on bereavement is *The Year of Magical Thinking*. Thanks to Faber, too, for permission to include an extract from Rachel Cusk's memoir, *Aftermath: On Marriage and Separation*. Cusk told the *Guardian*'s Kate Kellaway that 'Autobiography is increasingly the only form in all the arts. Description and character are dead', and that 'the idea of making up John and Jane and having them do things together seems utterly ridiculous'. She mentioned Karl Ove Knausgård, who has famously chronicled his own life in a series of novels collectively titled *My Struggle*. Sheila Heti took autobiographical writing in new directions with *How Should a Person Be*, a work of 'constructed reality', in her words, containing verbatim emails and transcribed conversations. Heti told art critic Dave Hickey it was 'tiresome to make up a fake person and put them through the paces of a fake story' in *The Believer* in 2007. Disillusionment with fiction on the page may not be unconnected with its growing success on screen; nowadays we look to television for the kind of epic stories we once got from novels. ('No one's writing *War and Peace*,' a publisher told me recently.)

'One can use one's life as material', said Elizabeth Bishop, so long as there's no violation of trust. Some relationships too sensitive to be treated in non-fiction find their way into prose. I gave as examples Harold Pinter's *Betrayal*, a play inspired by his affair with the journalist and television presenter Joan Bakewell, and Graham Greene's *The End of the Affair*, which drew on his long relationship with Catherine Walston. I could also have mentioned Hanif Kureishi's *Intimacy*. Greene's novel is set around Clapham Common, and I often think about it when I'm walking there and pass the house where he lived until bomb damage forced him out in 1940. On the same walk I can pass Angela Carter's house and remember the Gothic tales contained in *The Bloody Chamber*. Elizabeth Smart's *By Grand Central Station I Sat Down and Wept* is also inspired by a relationship, this time with poet George Barker. He wrote about the affair too and later their son Christopher Barker wrote about the misery of living with both of them. In a neat illustration of the way art keeps handing itself on, the Smiths have borrowed lines from Smart's novel in various songs and for the album title *Louder Than Bombs*.

The joy of writing about authors is that you get to celebrate your favourites. I could never single one out, but there are writers I enjoy for their style and writers I love for their ability to tell a story. Zora Neale Hurston's *Their Eyes Were Watching God* is an example of the first, Philip Roth's

American Pastoral of the second. For a bolt of creativity I sometimes reread the first paragraph of John Updike's *Rabbit, Run*, one of the best openings of any novel I know. I have reservations about both Roth and Updike, mostly to do with the credibility of their female characters – but a good reading relationship has room for caveats. For their excellent humour, as well as their excellent writing, I love Zadie Smith and Gabriel García Márquez. Smith's passage about the fervour that accompanies writing when it's going well comes from *Changing My Mind: Occasional Essays*. García Márquez described the pleasure of telling a story as 'the human condition that most resembles levitation' in his prologue to *Strange Pilgrims*. I'm grateful to be able to include an excerpt from John Irving's *The Hotel New Hampshire*, which has sad connotations for me, although many people love it. Al Alvarez's *The Savage God: A Study of Suicide* is a difficult but instructive read, and includes a chapter on Sylvia Plath.

Some writers are masters of style *and* story, such as Alan Hollinghurst in *The Line of Beauty*, or William Trevor, whose characters are so believable you wouldn't be surprised to meet them in a supermarket queue; many thanks to Penguin for allowing me to use an extract from Trevor's story 'Widows', which can be found in *William Trevor: The Collected Stories*. Jorge Luis Borges, often described as the father of modern Latin American fiction, wrote several stories I've mentioned in this book, all from *Fictions*, translated by Andrew Hurley. Among various observations on

James Joyce, Borges described *Ulysses* as an inspiration for 'Funes the Memorious' in *Jorge Luis Borges: Conversations*. Clarice Lispector is unique in her ability to swing from lightheartedness to horror in the space of a few sentences. I recommend her novel *The Passion According to G. H.*

If I could wake up tomorrow with the skills of just one writer, it would be Alice Munro. I study her sentences the way amateur magicians watch magic tricks. My copy of *Hateship, Friendship, Courtship, Loveship, Marriage* has fallen apart from devoted reading.

Is it possible to learn to write like one of the best? There are countless good books on the subject, not to mention all kinds of courses. I've quoted here from A. L. Kennedy's *On Writing* and Vladimir Nabokov's *Lectures on Literature*. Everything Zadie Smith says on the subject feels funny and true. Flannery O'Connor proposed that the teacher's work be 'largely negative' in *Mystery and Manners: Occasional Prose* (she also quipped 'There's many a best-seller that could have been prevented by a good teacher').

The research carried out by Andrew Piper and Richard Jean So, comparing writers who had taken a Master of Fine Arts in creative writing with ones who hadn't, was discussed in *The Atlantic Magazine*; Paul J. Zak's observation of the 'neural ballet' that takes place in our minds when we follow a story appeared in *Harvard Business Review*. Mark McGurl's *The Program Era: Postwar Fiction and the Rise of Creative Writing* is a mine of information on the growing popularity of creative writing in the USA, including the role of educator

Barrett Wendell, who may have been the first person to use that term 'creative writing', or at least to package it for teaching purposes. Katherine Dunn's short story 'The Resident Poet' appeared in the *New Yorker* in May 2020. Other anecdotes about writers' desire, thwarted and otherwise, came from *Yaddo: Making American Culture*. David Foster Wallace lamented his failure to get laid on tour to David Lipsky in *Although of Course You End Up Becoming Yourself*.

The figure of Antigone flits through the pages of this book, my identification with her as a teenager having made her both a threat and a talisman. I read a great deal about the classical figure some people see as a female cultural counterpart to Oedipus, and never quite decided whether she was a principled young woman bent on defending her brother's dignity, or a dogmatist bound to theology. The popularity of Sophocles' play – it is the most frequently performed Greek tragedy, with productions going on around the world at any given time – shows that she lends herself to different interpretations. Among other texts, I read George Eliot's essay 'The Antigone and Its Moral', Judith Butler's *Antigone's Claim: Kinship Between Life and Death*, and Helen Morales' *Antigone Rising*. Jean Anouilh's play *Antigone* was the version impressed on me at school. Since then I have also read versions by Seamus Heaney (*The Burial at Thebes: Sophocles' Antigone*), Tom Paulin (*The Riot Act*), Bertolt Brecht (*Antigone*, translated by Judith Malina) and Anne Carson (*Antigonick*). Carson also writes about Antigone in her collection of poems *Men in the Off Hours*.

I'm personally very grateful to Adam Thorpe, for his correspondence and for permission to print his poem 'Defeat', from *Birds with a Broken Wing* (Cape Poetry). I would also like to thank the various colleagues I have taught alongside, and learned from, and the Royal Literary Fund, an institution that does so much to support writers and to foster good writing in all kinds of organizations. Many thanks, too, to my agent Patrick Walsh and my editor Sarah Castleton for their invaluable suggestions and improvements, and heartfelt gratitude to Caroline Knight, Phoebe Carney and the team at Corsair.

Alvarez, Al, *The Savage God: A Study of Suicide*, Weidenfeld and Nicolson, London, 1971

Anouilh, Jean, *Antigone* trans. Barbara Bray, Bloomsbury, London, 2000

Bertolt Brecht, *Antigone*, trans. Judith Malina, Applause Books, New York, 1984

Borges, Jorge Luis, 'The Library of Babel', *Fictions*, trans. Andrew Hurley, Penguin, London, 2000

Burgin, Richard (ed.), *Jorge Luis Borges: Conversations*, University Press of Mississippi, Jackson, 1998

Butler, Judith, *Antigone's Claim: Kinship Between Life and Death*, Columbia University Press, New York, 2002

Carson, Anne, *Antigonick*, illustrated by Bianca Stone, Bloodaxe Books, Hexham, Northumberland, 2012

Carson, Anne, *Men in the Off Hours*, Cape, London, 2000

Carter, Angela, *The Bloody Chamber, and Other Stories*, Gollancz, London, 1979

Cheever, John, *The Journals*, Cape, London, 1991

Cusk, Rachel, *Aftermath: On Marriage and Separation*, Faber and Faber Ltd, London, 2019

Cusk, Rachel, 'Aftermath was creative death. I was heading into total silence', interview with Kate Kellaway in the *Guardian*, London, 24 August 2014

Dickens, Charles, 'Night Walks with the Uncommercial Traveller', *All the Year Round*, vol. 3, 21 July 1860, p. 350

Didion, Joan, *The Year of Magical Thinking*, Knopf, New York, 2005

Dunn, Katherine, 'The Resident Poet', *New Yorker* 11 May 2020

Eliot, George, 'The Antigone and Its Moral', *Leader*, vol. VII, 29 March 1856, p. 306

Flett, Kathryn, 'By Waterloo Station I Sat Down and Wept', *Observer*, February 1997

Frost, Robert, 'The Road Not Taken', *Mountain Interval*, Henry Holt, New York, 1916

García Márquez, Gabriel, *Strange Pilgrims* trans. Edith Grossman, Cape, London, 1993

Greene, Graham, *The End of the Affair*, Vintage Classics, London, 2019

Hamilton, Saskia (ed.), *The Dolphin Letters, 1970–1979: Elizabeth Hardwick, Robert Lowell, and Their Circle*, Faber and Faber Ltd, London, 2020

Heaney, Seamus, 'Blackberry Picking', *Opened Ground: Poems 1966–1996*, Faber and Faber Ltd, London, 2002

Heaney, Seamus, *The Burial at Thebes: Sophocles' Antigone*, Faber and Faber Ltd, London, 2011

Heti, Sheila, *How Should A Person Be*, Harvill Secker, London, 2013

Heti, Sheila, interview with Dave Hickey in *The Believer*, San Francisco, Issue 49, 1 November 2007

Hollinghurst, Alan, *The Line of Beauty*, Picador, London, 2004

Hurston, Zora Neale, *Their Eyes Were Watching God*, Virago, London, 1986

Irving, John, *The Hotel New Hampshire*, Cape, London, 1981

Jamie, Kathleen 'A Lone Enraptured Male' (review of Robert Macfarlane's *The Wild Places*) *London Review of Books*, vol. 30 no. 5, 6 March 2008

Kennedy, A. L., *On Writing*, extracts from blogpost VII, Cape, 2013

Knausgård, Karl Ove, *A Death in the Family: My Struggle*, trans. Don Bartlett, Harvill Secker, London, 2012

Kureishi, Hanif, *Intimacy*, Faber and Faber Ltd, London, 1998

Leader, Zachary (ed.), *On Life-Writing*, OUP, Oxford, 2015

Lipsky, David, *Although of Course You End Up Becoming Yourself: A Road Trip with David Foster Wallace*, Broadway Books, New York, 2010

Lispector, Clarice, *The Passion According to G. H.*, trans. Idra Novey, Penguin Classics, London, 2014

Loftus, Elizabeth, 'Misfortunes of Memory', *Philosophical Transactions of the Royal Society of London B*, vol. 2, issue 1110, 11 August 1983

Lowell, Robert, *The Dolphin, Two Versions, 1972–1973*, Farrar, Straus and Giroux, New York, 2019

Macdonald, Helen, *H is for Hawk*, Cape, London, 2014

McGee, Micki (ed.), *Yaddo: Making American culture*, The New York Public Library, New York, 2008

McGurl, Mark, *The Program Era: Postwar Fiction and the Rise of Creative Writing*, Harvard University Press, Cambridge, Massachusetts, 2009

Morales, Helen, *Antigone Rising: The Subversive Power of the Ancient Myths*, Wildfire, London, 2020

Munro, Alice, *Hateship, Friendship, Courtship, Loveship, Marriage*, Vintage, London, 2001

Nabokov, Vladimir, *Lectures on Literature*,
    Weidenfeld and Nicolson, London, 1980
O'Connor, Flannery, *Mystery and Manners: Occasional
    Prose*, Faber and Faber Ltd, London, 1972
Pack, Robert, *The Long View: Essays on the
    Discipline of Hope and Poetic Craft*, University of
    Massachusetts Press, Amherst,1992
Paulin, Tom, *The Riot Act: A Version of Sophocles'
    Antigone*, Faber and Faber Ltd, London, 1985
Pinter, Harold, *Betrayal*, Eyre Methuen,
    London, 1978
Piper, Andrew and Richard Jean So, 'How Has the
    MFA Changed the Contemporary Novel?' *The
    Atlantic Magazine*, 6 March 2016
Plath, Sylvia, 'Sheep in Fog', *Ariel*, Faber and Faber
    Ltd, London, 1965
Plath, Sylvia, *The Journals of Sylvia Plath, 1950–1962*,
    ed. Karen V. Kukil, Faber and Faber Ltd,
    London, 2000
Raine, Craig, 'Gethsemane', *Collected Poems 1978–
    1999*, Picador, London, 2000
Roth, Philip, *American Pastoral*, Vintage Classics,
    London, 2019
Sage, Lorna, *Bad Blood*, Fourth Estate,
    London, 2001
Schachtel, Ernest, 'On Memory and Childhood
    Amnesia', *Psychiatry*, 1947, vol. 10, issue 1,
    pp. 1–26

Seamus Heaney and the Music of What Happens, BBC documentary, first aired 30 November, 2019

Shaine Cunningham, Laura *Sleeping Arrangements*, Bloomsbury, London, 2006

Smart, Elizabeth, *By Grand Central Station I Sat Down and Wept*, Flamingo, London, 1992

Smith, Zadie, *Feel Free*, Penguin, London, 2018

Smith, Zadie, *Changing My Mind: Occasional Essays*, Penguin, London, 2009

Thorpe, Adam, 'Defeat', *Birds with a Broken Wing*, Cape, London, 2007

Trevor, William, 'Widows', in *William Trevor: The Collected Stories*, Penguin, London, 2003

Twain, Mark, *Roughing It*, American Publishing Company, Hartford, Connecticut, 1872

Updike, John, *Rabbit, Run*, Penguin, London, 2006

Winter, Alison, *Memory: Fragments of a Modern History*, University of Chicago Press, Chicago, 2012

Woolf, Virginia, 'Street Haunting', *Yale Review*, 1927

Woolf, Virginia, 'The Oxford Street Tide', essay written for *Good Housekeeping Magazine* 1931–32, published in *The London Scene: Five Essays by Virginia Woolf*, Frank Hallman, New York, 1975.

Woolf, Virginia, *A Writer's Diary: Being Extracts from the Diary of Virginia Woolf*, ed. Leonard Woolf, Persephone Books, London, 2012

Zak, Paul J., 'Why Your Brain Loves Good
    Storytelling', *Harvard Business Review*, 28
    October 2014